PRAISE FOR 'ST

"A fantastic read – certainly something all senior and middle leaders should have on their book shelves and read not just once but many times! It ought to be a mandatory part of the NPQH reading list."
Andrew Parkin, Principal, St Dominic's Sixth Form College, London

"This book is wise, timely and very well needed by the profession; it is reassuring, re-affirming and motivating. It's so rare to have the human experience of being a school leader really explored in a perceptive, emotionally intelligent but equally incisive and challenging way. I hope others read this and are as encouraged as I was."
Kathryn Pugh, Headteacher, The St Marylebone CE School, London

"I loved reading Staying A Head! It acknowledges just how tough the role of headship is. I felt reassured that I am doing a good job. It offers so many strategies to reflect on and develop your practice. It is an excellent read and comes highly recommended to any school leader, irrespective of where they are on their journey. A series of coaching sessions in a book! Perfect."
Alison Kriel, Headteacher, Northwold Primary School, London

STAYING A HEAD
The Stress Management Secrets
of Successful School Leaders

Dedicated to my children Isaac, Curtis-Ray and Lauren; my constant source of love, hope and inspiration.

STAYING A HEAD
The Stress Management Secrets of Successful School Leaders

Viv Grant

Published in 2014 by Integrity Coaching

Staying A Head
The Stress Management Secrets of Successful School Leaders

First published in 2014 by
Integrity Coaching
4 Abercrombie Street,
London, SW11 2JD
www.integritycoaching.co.uk

Cover design by Spiffing Covers
www.spiffingcovers.com

Illustrations: Sye Watts
www.syewatts.co.uk

Typeset by EPLS Design
www.eplsdesign.com

This book is printed on demand so no copies will be
remaindered or pulped

ISBN 978-0-9929250-0-0

ACKNOWLEDGEMENTS

I will be forever grateful to every single school leader that I have had the privilege to coach. This book exists because you had the courage to share the true realities of what it takes to be a successful school leader with me. Thank you for staying true to your vision and true to yourselves. I know that for as long as you remain in the positions that you are in, our children's futures are safe in your hands.

I also want to thank members of my family, friends and colleagues who in one way or another have supported me in the writing of this book. In particular:

Tristram Pye, Millicent Grant, Venetia Grant, Yannick Mango, Olusola Oyeleye, Benjamin Washington, Francis Dickens, Peter Milligan, Andrew Ceresa, Kathryn Lovewell, Herman Stewart, Maria Hampshire, Maria Ilia and Jack Jewell.

Your support across the different stages of writing this book has been invaluable and has meant the world to me.

There are numerous others who have influenced me and have had an impact on who I am now as an author and coach. Those who trod the path with me in my early days as a teacher, others who believed in me and saw things in me that I didn't always see in myself as I moved into school leadership, and those at the London Centre for Leadership in Learning, who first introduced me to the gentle power of coaching as tool for school improvement. Thank you.

It would probably take another chapter in itself if I were to list the names of all those who have been with me at these different stages of my journey. Suffice to say, if you read this book and recognise your influence, know that my love and gratitude goes out to you also.

CONTENTS

Developing a systematic way to help teachers get better is the most powerful idea in education today. The surest way to weaken it is to twist it into a capricious exercise in public shaming. Let's focus on creating a personnel system that truly helps teachers to improve.

Bill Gates

FOREWORD

Every choice made by a school leader, from managing a conflict situation to choosing to work late, has a direct impact on the school staff and consequently on the children. This book, *Staying A Head*, is a timely reminder for every school leader that their thoughts, words, feelings and actions are pivotal to the smooth running and happiness of their school; their influential position in society carries great responsibility and often brings a great personal burden.

In *Staying A Head*, Viv Grant gently unravels the personal and professional needs of school leaders in their highly pressured, and often isolating, role. She brings humanity back into what can be a dehumanising fear-based environment.

Viv's own experiences as a Headteacher, and now as an executive coach, enable her to guide her readers powerfully to a place of self-enquiry for effective leadership. She challenges the masks many school leaders wear to cover up their anxiety and self-doubt, especially when they are first in their role. She rightly encourages them to investigate their negative mind chatter, their comfort zones and their people management skills to facilitate both personal and professional evolution.

School leaders are not bullet-proof, even when they appear to be. *Staying A Head* supports each leader to take time out to reflect, acknowledge their vulnerability, and in turn develop their self-esteem to build new levels of confidence from within.

Headteachers are the North Star in the sky of education – the guiding force of their school. They light the way for their teaching team and help each member of that team to shine brightly in an often dark sky. With coaching support, Viv demonstrates how Headteachers and other senior leaders can reframe the teaching darkness by recognising that stars cannot be seen or enjoyed without the darkness that falls at night.

She shows with compassion and non-judgement that there is a way through the jungle of internal and external pressures. She brings hope, inspiration and constructive guidance to people in a highly complex position within the community.

Our school leaders must give themselves permission to ask for help, and to receive support from a neutral source. Then – and only then – the unhelpful cycle of self-sacrifice can be addressed. Every parent wants healthy and happy teachers in front of their children. School leaders must therefore model best practice – not by employing a façade of capability and working themselves into the ground, but by adopting an authentic, confident and mindful approach to relationships, self-care and governance.

All Olympic gold medallists have coaches. 'Education athletes' also require encouragement, reassurance and support; they have many hurdles to jump and many miles to run, and they need hours and hours of unseen training to ensure they are fit for the track. Every member of staff and every child relies on their leader to take them to the finishing line. Sadly, many school leaders and Headteachers in particular, rarely have a team of cheerleaders to spur them on. This is why *Staying A Head* is so valuable in the current school climate. Coaches enable leaders of education to warm up, flex their muscles and try new techniques and approaches in their thinking, so that they are fit and ready for the competition to come.

Education is competitive! League tables and exam results place school leaders under constant pressure to perform and ensure their school meets – or exceeds – targets. Effective leaders who are under incessant pressure need to be emotionally resilient, confident in themselves and their choices, and be able to demonstrate courage in the face of adversity. They must deal with uncertainty, manage conflict and overcome emotive situations, both inside and outside the school, while maintaining a positive outlook.

This is why coaching is so valuable to school leaders. It provides a safe space to unearth, explore and respond to internal and external challenges. It is a 'healthy antidote to the pressures of school life'.

Staying A Head will ease you out of your comfort zone and support you in the 'stretch zone'. As with all great coaching, it will highlight the benefits of being stretched while insisting on a compassionate approach to your doubts and fears. With Viv, you will appreciate how the relationship between leader and coach ensures you will bend (not break) under the constant changes and demands of leadership.

Staying A Head will help you stay true to your vision and true to yourself. It will show you how to keep your deep, burning passion alive without sacrificing yourself. It will encourage you to know yourself and therefore get the best out of yourself as a leader. In turn, it will help you get the best out of your staff. It will inspire the translation of your school development plan through self-development.

This book reveals the untapped potential of coaching for school leaders for personal and professional growth. Your author stands at the chalk face – she knows what the reality of being a school leader is, and offers you a step-by-step guide to discovering your natural leadership skills. This book will restore the magic of your leadership life.

Thank you for loving your staff and children enough to put yourself first. You are the jewel in the crown of education. This is an opportunity to polish your diamond!

To your good health and happiness,

Kathryn Lovewell (author of *Every Teacher Matters*)

INTRODUCTION

Does leading have to be at such a great personal cost to myself?

This was the question that stayed with me throughout my career as a Headteacher. And it is the question I know many Headteachers and senior school leaders ask themselves today. It may be the very reason you've picked up this book, because you're seeking a solution that will help you overcome the inherent stresses of your role as a school leader.

I hope I can help. This book is not meant to be a 'heavy' read. I have no intention of adding to your already considerable workload, but I do hope to provide you with an easy-to-read, practical guidebook that will help you:

(a) to understand your own unique experience of what it means for you to be a school leader, and
(b) to develop tools to enable you to develop a greater sense of control, self-belief and emotional resilience.

This book has been written with the intention of filling the gap that existed when I was a Headteacher. Actually, it was more than a gap – it was a gaping chasm into which I poured all my deepest, darkest thoughts and fears. And every morning, I built a bridge to cross over it, so that I could perform effectively in my role as Headteacher. Depending on the stress of the day, or the week, and how I was feeling, that bridge sometimes felt incredibly sturdy and strong. At other times it felt weak and fragile, like an ancient, decaying rope bridge in one of those all-action adventure movies.

Figure A: Rope bridge

It wasn't until I left headship to work on national programmes, supporting and developing both aspiring and established Headteachers, that I realised I hadn't been alone. It wasn't just heads who were newly in post that opened up to me; established colleagues also shared their stories about the true cost of school leadership. A current head of an inner London primary school recently said to me: *'I've been working in inner-city schools for twenty-eight years – fourteen as a Headteacher. Nothing prepares you for headship; the realisation that the buck stops with you, the weight of the responsibility for a community that believes and trusts that whatever the problem, you can fix it.*

We spend our days surrounded by pupils, staff, parents – their joy, their anger, their fear. We sway from highs to lows, joyous moments to deep sadness, from success to managing failure. We face fear and courage on our own, and there are few opportunities to show our own vulnerability. We share different issues with different people in a measured way – we don't want to burden anyone.

We are paid to carry the load; it's the responsibility of the job. As a consequence, no one else is the keeper of the whole school picture. It sets us apart and leads to overwhelming feelings of loneliness – despite being in constant demand. Outwardly we model calm, order,

*positivity, but as the capacity to cope diminishes, over time
we become over-absorbed by school life and detached from
our own feelings and relationships.'*

It was through listening to accounts such as these that I
realised statutory leadership training is simply not enough.
There is something unique about stepping into the role
of a senior school leader and – if your career path takes
you even further – to that of Headteacher. There is a need
to learn how to manage the intense demands of both the
operational and strategic aspects of the role, as well as the
huge range of emotions (your own and others') that are the
flip-side of being a leader.

Extract from my diary from March 2001

It hasn't been the best of weeks. My Year 6 teacher is still out ill, and
the supply teacher we had booked to cover her class has been in a
road accident and is in intensive care. The father of another member
of staff has just died and today she broke down in tears in my office.
Despite trying everything to help Craig to manage his anger, I had to
exclude him for a couple of days. On Wednesday, he had an enormous
temper tantrum, swore at everyone in sight and smashed our new
glass 'child-proof' entrance doors to pieces. Despite the fact that
I've taken my school out of special measures and had my leadership
praised by OFSTED, it hasn't made the slightest bit of difference to how
I'm feeling inside. Everyone turns to me; I have to carry everyone and
everything. Right now, I just feel that it's all too much. I am tired of
being tired. I am tired of giving every day. I am exhausted!

My role feels all-consuming and I feel very alone. There seems to
be no one I can go to in confidence:

- when things go wrong
- to talk through difficult situations with
- to reflect on the week and what has occurred for me
- to help me review my vision for the school and my life.

I love this school, I love my staff, and I love the children, but does
leading have to be at such a great personal cost to myself?

So ... Who is this book for?

This book is for any senior school leader who truly believes they can make a big difference to the lives of the children in their school, and who wants to understand how their vision can be achieved at the same time as keeping a clear focus on maintaining their own emotional and mental health and well-being.

I firmly believe that a passion for excellence, rigour and high standards for all should sit alongside compassion, humanity and hope. These values should never be mutually exclusive.

No school leader should regularly be in a position in which they have to cross a fragile bridge every morning just to get to work. Your role as leader is too valuable. It is the future of your children that is at stake. If the frayed rope bridge is not repaired, if your inner resources are not fortified, sooner or later the bridge will snap, and with it the vision that you had for yourself and your school.

If you are going to cross that bridge, this book will help you to develop the inner resources to get to the other side. Imagine that each morning before you go to work, you pack a rucksack with four essential pieces of equipment, which not only serve to get you through each day, but also:

- nurture you
- support you
- encourage you, and
- fortify you.

If you are familiar with the work of Daniel Goleman, you will be familiar with the following four components of emotional intelligence. These are adapted from *Primal Leadership: The Hidden Driver of Great Performance* (Goleman, 2003a).

1. Self-awareness

This is the ability to read your own emotions. It is a competency that allows people to know their strengths and limitations, and feel confident about their self-worth. Effective school leaders use self-awareness to gauge their own moods accurately and to know intuitively how they are affecting others.

2. Self-management

This relates to your ability to control your emotions and act with honesty and integrity in reliable and adaptable ways. Effective school leaders don't let an occasional bad mood seize the day. They use self-management to leave their bad moods outside the school gates, or to explain the origin of their mood to others in a reasonable manner.

3. Social awareness

This includes the key capabilities of empathy and organisational intuition. School leaders with a high level of social awareness do more than sense other people's emotions – they show that they care. They also understand the 'politics' of their school and the wider context, thus they understand how their words and actions make others feel, and they are sensitive enough to change them when their impact is negative.

4. Relationship management

This addresses our ability to communicate clearly and convincingly, to disarm conflicts, and to build strong personal bonds. Effective school leaders use these skills to spread their enthusiasm and solve disagreements, often with humour and kindness.

These four attributes are needed by all successful school leaders if they are to survive and thrive. If you have been in a senior leadership role for a while and have attended various leadership training programmes, I'm sure you will have completed some sort of emotional intelligence assessment, or undertaken a workshop or two. However, I'm sure you can testify that such assessments and workshops are only the beginning. Experience teaches us that raising our level of emotional intelligence is often a very personal and private process. We develop these competencies and strengthen our ability to use them only when we develop ways of being that enable us to understand how our thoughts, feelings and behaviours impact upon the vision we have for ourselves and our relationships with others.

What role does coaching play in all of this?

Much of what we hear about coaching in the education sector focuses on the mechanics of the process. Coaching is quite often seen simply as a tool for guiding a conversation, whereby an individual is supported to take ownership of his or her particular issue and find an appropriate solution for addressing it. As important as this process is, there is so much more to coaching.

In the right environment, coaching can support the growth of the inner self. It can help individuals to come to understand themselves and meet themselves on different terms. Through questioning, reflection and dialogue, coaching helps school leaders develop resilience, insight and courage – all part and parcel of developing Goleman's core emotional attributes.

This book will help you develop your core emotional intelligence. It has been written to provide you with a deeper understanding of the role that coaching can play in your life as a school leader. Had I discovered coaching when I was a Headteacher, I believe my experience of the role would have been very different. My diary entries would not have been about my fears and worries; they would have been about coaching, and how it helped me:

- Develop a greater understanding of who I was as a person.
- Identify the personal and professional attributes I needed to develop in order to be the kind of leader I wanted to be.
- Increase my emotional intelligence and my ability to maintain my own emotional, spiritual and mental well-being.
- Develop reflective practices for maximising my own performance and the performance of others.

As you know, this was not my experience unfortunately, but it is my hope that by reading this book it will be yours.

BOOK OVERVIEW

I'd like you to view this book as a practical companion for supporting you in your role. As you read, take a pencil or highlighter and mark anything on the pages that you feel is relevant to you. A good coach will always ask you questions, so keep these three key questions in mind as you read (perhaps recording your responses in a notebook):

1. What does this mean for me?
2. How can this help me to develop in my role as a school leader?
3. What are the action steps that I need to take in order to reduce my stress levels and experience greater fulfilment in my role?

Chapter 1: Meeting emotional needs
The book begins by helping you to understand exactly what our basic human emotional needs are, and why they need to be satisfied in order for us to have lives that are mentally and emotionally healthy.

Chapter 2: Overcoming loneliness at the top
This chapter explores why leadership can be such a lonely place. It considers the current educational landscape, the lack of external support mechanisms that contribute to feelings of isolation, and what actions can be taken to lessen feelings of isolation and loneliness.

Chapter 3: Understanding self
Here, we consider why all school leaders must know and understand themselves. Nathaniel Branden, an American psychotherapist, noted that:

Leaders often do not fully recognise the extent to which who they are affects virtually every aspect of their organisation.
Branden (1994)

I have found this to be true for many school leaders, which is why this chapter explores how greater self-understanding leads to greater personal and professional fulfilment.

Chapter 4: Learning to drop the leadership mask
This chapter focuses on precisely what school leaders need to prevent them from losing sight of their own humanity. This includes the human behaviour theory of 'dramaturgy', a termed coined by sociologist Erving Goffman in the 1960s with respect to how school leaders perform in front of different audiences.

Chapter 5: Moving out of comfort zones
This chapter explores the actions that school leaders need to take in order to grow, not just themselves but also those they lead and manage. It considers the limitations that fear places on their actions and how such fear can be overcome, to produce a more self-confident approach to school leadership.

Chapter 6: Decluttering the mind
A practical guide to the art of coaching is presented in this chapter. Along with a theoretical overview of the coaching process, it describes a level of understanding that will enable you to apply basic coaching skills and principles to your everyday life.

Chapter 7: Bringing out the best in others
This discussion focuses on working with those you lead and manage, to maximise their potential. It will help you understand how to manage yourself better when dealing with staff, and how to develop your performance management processes to bring out the best in them.

Chapter 8: Keeping hope alive

The closing chapter describes seven key leadership lessons for sustaining hope and keeping school leaders connected with their core values, their vision and their purpose.

There are exercises in some of the chapters. These will invite you to stop, pause and reflect on what you have read. Allow yourself time to complete them, so that you develop a deeper understanding of your own personal leadership journey and the actions you should take to lead a more balanced life as a school leader.

PROLOGUE

Begin with the end in mind
Covey (1989)

I don't know where you are on your leadership journey. You may be thinking about taking on a new senior leadership post, or you may be well established in the role, with many years' experience under your belt. What I do know is that wherever you are on that journey (and you may think I am a little crazy for saying this) you need to put *yourself first*.

That's right. I said: *PUT YOURSELF FIRST.*

Not the children, not the teachers, not the parents, not the governors – YOU! In asking you to put yourself first, I am not asking you to adopt selfish, ego-driven behaviours; I'm simply asking you to prioritise the meeting of your own needs as a human being, because only when your own needs have been met are you able to meet the needs of others.

Why am I asking you to do this? Too often, school leaders (in particular, Headteachers) start with the end in mind for their schools, without a moment's thought for what achievement of that end result might mean for them on a personal or professional level. Too often, the end result means burn-out; at best, it means tiredness and disillusionment with the role.

When you take those initial steps into school leadership, you begin a process of personal transformation. You may find that this is a process for which you are surprisingly ill-prepared, despite your years of training and experience. Many school leaders find that the twinned processes of school and personal transformation are fraught with difficulties. Left to struggle alone, many only achieve a fraction of what might have been possible had they been given the right type of spiritual, mental and emotional support for the journey.

So learn to put yourself first. You can begin that journey today by taking a step back from the current demands and pressures of your role. The process of school transformation is a deeply personal process; one that requires you to be fully conscious of who you are as a person, and the changes that are occurring both in and around you as you seek to bring the vision for your school to life.

Are you ready?

I'd like you to pause for a moment and imagine that today is your first day in a new senior leadership role. If you are about to take up your post, this is a great exercise to do. If you have been a senior leader for a while, then there is a lot to be gained from reflecting on the past, where you are now, and what you would do differently. Take a pen or a pencil and before you read any further, complete the personal and professional balance wheels on the following pages.

Begin with the end in mind: exactly what do you want your personal and professional goals to look like?

How to complete your professional life wheel

Vision
Clarify your vision for your end goal for your school. Think deeply about the vision you have for your school, or the school that you hope to lead one day. Write that vision in the centre of the wheel. Include as much detail as possible. What will you see, hear or feel that will tell you that your vision has been achieved? If you prefer, you can draw your image of the future – whatever will be of most use to you.

Goals
Set goals that are aligned to the fulfilment of the vision you have for your school; they will be fulfilled through people and the relationships you build with them. So for each segment of the wheel nearest to your vision, write down a key personnel or human-process goal that will need to be achieved in order for your school vision to become a reality. How do you want your senior leadership team to operate? What type of relationship do you want with your governors? What level of support will you need from your admin team?

Action
Decide on the actions needed to bring your goals and vision to life. In the outer rim, next to each goal, write very clearly the specific action steps that you will need to take.

Figure B: Professional life wheel

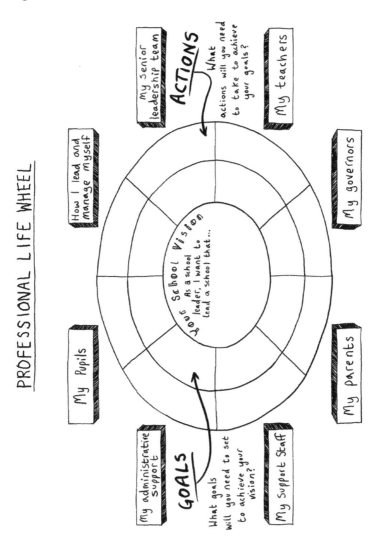

How to complete your personal life wheel

Vision

Clarify your vision regarding the end goal for you as a person. Skipping this part means you may achieve your vision for your school, but at a high personal cost to yourself. Think deeply about the vision you have for yourself as a person – the whole you; your life both inside and outside of school. Write that vision in the space in the centre of the wheel, giving as much detail as possible. What will you see, hear or feel that will tell you your vision has been achieved? Again, if you prefer, draw a picture of your imagined future.

Goals

Set yourself goals that are aligned to the vision of what you want for yourself as a person. For each segment of the wheel nearest to your personal vision, write down key personal goals that will need to be achieved in order for your personal goals to become a reality. How much time do you want to be able to pursue your hobbies? What type of relationship do you want with those who are nearest and dearest to you?

Action

Decide on the actions required to bring your goals and vision to life. In the outer rim next to each goal, write very clearly the specific action steps you will need to take.

Figure C: Personal life wheel

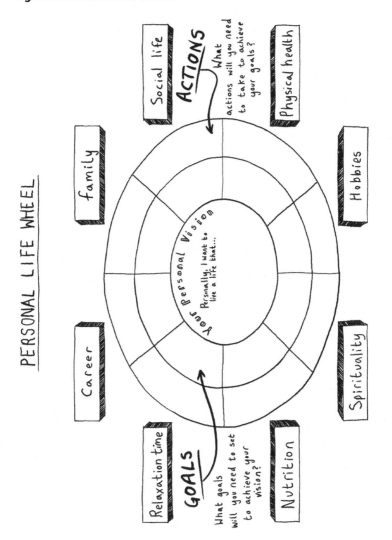

STOP, PAUSE AND REFLECT

Now reflect on the following questions:

- How well-aligned are your wheels when you compare them side by side?
- As a school leader, how can you ensure that your role does not impact negatively on the personal goals you have for yourself?
- What will it take for you to achieve satisfaction on both a professional and personal level?
- Who else needs to understand what your goals are in both areas of your life, and how can they support you?
- What are the changes or actions you will need to take to ensure that you lead a balanced life as a school leader?

You may not be able to answer all of the questions now. That's okay. By the time you reach the end of this book, you may have a much clearer idea of what you need to do. For now, I just want you to be mindful of the fact that if you are more conscious of your desired outcomes, both on a personal and professional level, then you are far more likely to be able to make the choices that will enable you to live a more congruent and balanced life as a school leader.

CHAPTER 1:
Meeting Emotional Needs

Teachers need to be comfortable talking about feelings.

**Daniel Goleman
(author, psychologist and
science journalist)**

Meeting Emotional Needs

In this chapter you will find answers to the questions:
- What are our basic emotional needs?
- Why do school leaders need to have their emotional needs met?
- What are the consequences of unmet emotional needs?
- What role does empathic listening play in meeting emotional needs?

*HEADTEACHER FOUND DEAD IN BURNT-OUT
CAR AFTER 'SUICIDE'*
Mail online 2014

*HEADTEACHER KILLED HERSELF AFTER SIX MONTHS
IN JOB, CORONER RULES*
The Guardian 2013

*LEADERSHIP IS LIKE THE WIZARD OF OZ –
A FAÇADE THAT LACKS MAGIC*
The Guardian Teacher Network 2012

PUSHED TO THE BRINK
Times Education Supplement 2012

When we read newspaper headlines such as these, we know that something is desperately wrong with our education system. The current narrative surrounding school improvement, has become – to quote the words of Bill Gates – *'a capricious exercise in public shaming'.*

It is now a narrative that increasingly sets schools against one another. One by-product of this are increased feelings of emotional isolation within the education system. In such an environment, people lose the ability to form trusting relationships, and feelings of connectedness and shared self-worth are lost when schools find themselves pitted against each other for a position on government league tables.

External pressures—inner turmoil

I recently attended a well-being conference for school leaders. An OFSTED inspector was one of the guest speakers. As the present school leaders aired their feelings about the stress caused by the revised OFSTED framework, this inspector's demeanour changed. Initially he confidently told the audience how they must think and feel about the new arrangements, but he became nervous and agitated when the audience asked him to listen to their actual thoughts and feelings. It seemed that he was uncomfortable with the level of emotion in the room, and to have acknowledged that depth of feeling would have left him exposed and vulnerable. I believe that if he had dropped his guard – if only for a moment – he would have shown a more human side of OFSTED, which is what the delegates were desperate to see. Like all of us, they just wanted to be listened to.

When our emotional needs are not met, we feel dehumanised and alone. We feel as though our humanity has been pushed to one side. The ability to feel, to laugh, to cry, to hurt can all be seen as hindrances to one's ability to lead effectively. Without them, we damage not only our own, but also other people's, feelings of self-worth.

As Butler and Hope point out:

There is nothing so disabling as a sense of worthlessness. People who feel they are worthless ... feel that they have nothing to contribute. They hold themselves back and the prophecy becomes self-fulfilling.
Butler and Hope (2010)

We see this sense of worthlessness being played out in our schools every day. The OFSTED categories have become labels by which many school leaders define their own sense of self-worth. It shouldn't happen, but it does. We need to acknowledge that for as long as this continues to happen, individuals in schools with 'low' OFSTED categorisations of worth, will struggle to adopt the behaviours necessary to move them and their schools to higher feelings of self-worth. It is not impossible – there are schools all over the country that find the inner resolve necessary to improve their OFSTED rating – but we need to be honest and admit that the road to OFSTED success is often a tiring uphill journey. And for those school leaders who have to direct the footsteps of others, the journey is even more arduous because of the amount of emotional baggage (their own and others') they are forced to carry.

The consequences of emotional insensitivity

Many school leaders lead from a place of inner dissonance. Their basic emotional needs of feeling accepted, appreciated, believed in, respected, listened to, valued and supported are ignored. Many suffer alone, in silence, and thus lead from a place of hidden inner turmoil and self-doubt.

We all have basic human emotional needs (see Table 1), although the degree to which people require these needs to be met varies greatly. Our individual identities are dependent on our parenting and our life experiences and how both have shaped our sense of self. One person may need autonomy to feel in control; another may need approval and support from other people.

Table 1: Words relating to emotional needs that we need to have met:

Accepted	Listened to
Acknowledged	Loved
Admired	Needed
Appreciated	Noticed
Approved of	Powerful
Believed in	Private
Capable	Productive
Cared about	Reassured
Challenged	Recognised
Clear (not confused)	Respected
Competent	Safe and secure
Confident	Supported
Forgiven (and forgiving)	Treated fairly
Free	Trusted
Fulfilled	Understood (and
Heard	understanding)
Helped (and helpful)	Useful
Important	Valued
In control	Worthy
Included	

When these natural emotional needs are met, healthy behaviour follows. Just observe the children in your school. It is often clear whose needs are being met and whose are not. It is the same for adults. Our behaviours reveal the realities of our own inner worlds and the degree to which our own hidden emotional needs are being met.

Safeguarding the vulnerable self

When the emotional needs of school leaders are not met, it is their vulnerable self that suffers. Locked away behind a wall of self-preservation, and sometimes fear, individuals end up neglecting that part of themselves that needs to be truly listened to, nurtured and encouraged; that part of themselves that needs support so that they can grow fully into the vision that they have for themselves as a leader.

Where does all the emotional energy go?

Your role as a school leader requires an endless amount of energy. Energy is defined in the Oxford English dictionary as: The strength and vitality required for sustained physical or mental activity. However, you know from your own experience as a school leader, that the definition should also include 'sustained emotional activity.' When you are working in a school, engaging day-by-day with children and their families, teachers, support staff, governors and other adults, you know that you spend as much, if not more, energy meeting the emotional needs of others. As a result, you end up carrying a huge emotional debt and become increasingly emotionally overdrawn, with no readily identifiable means for bringing your emotional account back into credit.

School development is, therefore, also about emotional development. The ability to meet the emotional needs of others is central to the levels of effectiveness displayed by school leaders. The ability to do so is a requirement that increases during periods of stress.

What the problem is

Your preparation for becoming a school leader does not provide comprehensive training on understanding, and responding to, other people's emotional needs. Let's be honest, we often have enough trouble understanding our own! You may feel that you are a novice in the field of understanding human emotion, yet your role demands that you become an expert. This means that you give without receiving, and even when the well runs dry, you attempt to become a miracle worker, still trying to meet the needs of others when you have absolutely nothing left to give.

When we 'burn out' – when our emotional needs are left unmet – we experience mental and emotional exhaustion and derive less satisfaction from our lives. Feelings of self-doubt creep in, as do also harmful ways of meeting our unmet emotional needs. Whether that involves alcohol, food, smoking or some other type of self-medication, we human beings are adept at finding ways to squash the truth of what we are really feeling. We become so adept at it that sometimes we are oblivious to the fact that our habits and addictions are dampening our ability to be in tune with our emotions. We become used to living 'emotion-less' lives.

One Headteacher I worked with reflected on her habits before coaching. She said: *'For years, I had been doing what I do; not looking after myself, emotionally, mentally and spiritually. I had learned to ignore things that had had a negative impact on me.'*

The co-authors of *Resonant Leadership*, call this way of being the Sacrifice Syndrome. They say:

When leaders sacrifice too much for too long – and reap too little – they can become trapped in the Sacrifice Syndrome. Dissonance becomes the default.
Boyatzis and McKee (2005)

When I look back on my years as a Headteacher, and the work I do now with school leaders, I realise just how easy it is for symptoms of the Sacrifice Syndrome (Figure 1.1) to become the norm. During my time as a Headteacher, I came to accept tiredness, emotional overload and irritability as the norm. Nothing that I either observed or saw among my peers contradicted this perception; everyone was just so good at grandstanding that I believed we were all superhuman and had no need to have our emotional needs met.

Figure 1.1: The Sacrifice Syndrome

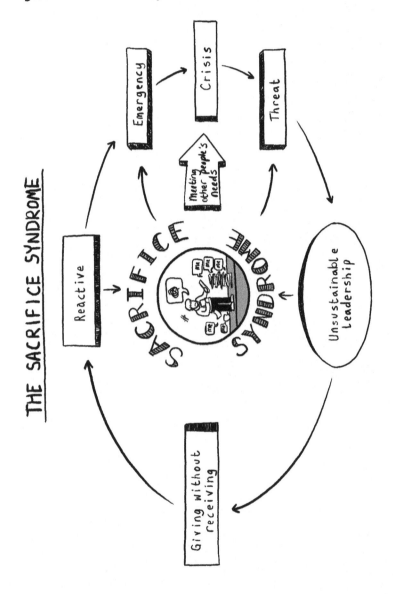

Yet despite buying into the myth, I can recall countless moments when I gave and I gave and I gave. There were moments when I cried from the sheer exhaustion of giving all of the time, but never stopped long enough to question the relationship between my inner emotional state and my outer performance as a leader. I just kept on going. Until one day...

I decided to make a home visit to one of our Year 6 pupils, Luke. I believed Luke was a star in the making. He had a winning smile and a wit and intelligence way beyond his 11 years. But there was a problem. There was nothing in his life outside school that told him he was special, that he could achieve his dreams and hopes for the future. He lived on a local estate which was soulless and depressing, like many other inner-city dwellings, and he lived in a home where love was regularly displaced by anger, retribution and fear. However, that wasn't going to stop me. I believed in Luke. I believed in what the future held for him. I believed that if we could get his mother onside, she would also come to believe in the vision I held for her son.

After another typical day of giving on top of my everyday duties, sorting out a raft of problematic staff issues, dealing with worrying child protection cases and seeking to meet the often conflicting 'urgent' needs of others, I went to visit Luke at home. I took a French-speaking colleague with me because his mother's first language was French. Within minutes of entering his flat, his mother hurled a torrent of abuse at me in a mixture of French and broken English. At seven o'clock in the evening, didn't I have better things to do with my time? Who the **** was I to come to her house and tell her how to raise her son? Rather than telling her what to do, shouldn't I be at home looking after my own son?

At that moment something inside me cracked. On another day, at another time, when I wasn't so tired, I may have found the inner resolve to stand my ground and speak up for Luke and the vision that I had for him and so desperately wanted her to see. But there and then, words failed me. Thankfully, my colleague spoke for me. She made our excuses and we left. We climbed into my car and, with the rain pouring down outside, I didn't just cry, I sobbed. I let go of the wall that I had built around my emotions and sobbed until there were no more tears left to cry.

Luke's mother's words had stung, but she was right. My priorities were skewed. I had equated putting the children of my school first, sacrificing my own life outside school and failing to meet my own responsibilities and needs as a parent with being an effective school leader. If I hadn't been so caught up in the endless round of giving and making less-than-conscious decisions, I would not have been in my car that night, emotionally spent.

If I had known how to spend more time 'being' and making conscious decisions, it is likely I would have arranged to see Luke's mother during the school day. Just perhaps she would have been more amenable and I would have had both the emotional and mental acuity to have a rational conversation with her about her son. However, such is the insidiousness of the Sacrifice Syndrome that before we know it, we are caught up in its vicious cycle. We unconsciously adopt ways of thinking and patterns of behaviour that often cause us more harm than good. It is not until something happens in our life and causes us to stop that we are forced to reflect and take notice of the consequences of our behaviours.

Sitting in my car that night, I felt an acute mixture of sadness, regret, loneliness, confusion, hurt and pain. This was not what I had expected headship to be about. Raising standards, fostering good teaching and learning, holding staff to account – yes; but the internal struggle between living according to one's own values and dealing with my own and others' emotional baggage – no. I definitely did not sign up for that.

Until that moment, my ability to grandstand had meant I had been able to hide my true feelings from myself as well as others. I was caught up in the Sacrifice Syndrome with no apparent way out. In an attempt to find solace, I turned to the counsellor who worked with some of the most vulnerable children in our school. I just needed someone to talk to, someone who did not require anything of me. Someone who would listen to me and not judge; someone who could create a space for me just to be myself. Not Viv Grant the Headteacher. Just me.

In finding someone 'neutral' to confide in and who was skilled as a listener, I was able to gradually find my footing and plot a way out of the Sacrifice Syndrome.

How close are you to the edge?

Stop for one moment and think about your own experience of being a leader. To what extent have you hidden the truth of what you are really feeling from yourself and others? What patterns of behaviour have you adopted that have helped to 'protect' you from the emotional toil of school leadership? Take a look at the following list of common symptoms of the Sacrifice Syndrome. If more than a few of these behaviours resonate with you, then it may be helpful to ask yourself:

- What is this telling me?
- What can I do about it?
- Do I want my life as a school leader to be defined by these behaviours?'

Common symptoms of the Sacrifice Syndrome

- Taking foolhardy risks
- Acting out of character
- Avoiding challenging situations
- Adopting a façade that all is well, even outside of work
- Becoming withdrawn
- Self-doubt
- Constant tiredness and irritability

- Inability to retain perspective
- Always assuming the worst possible outcome
- Not listening to your body
- Mentally, emotionally and physically pushing yourself
- Being reactive to situations, big and small
- Operating on 'auto-drive', allowing no time to think or process emotions
- Disconnecting from your own emotions and feelings
- Managing yourself and relationships from the 'head' and disengaging with your 'heart'

When energy levels are low and pressures are high, individuals do not see these types of behaviour as warning signals. Their measures of success become skewed. They begin to see success as simply getting to the end of each day – even if that means ending each day with a splitting headache. They have got through it. That's all that matters. Boyatsiz and McKee argue that:

Reversing the slide into dissonance and keeping yourself energised as a leader are only possible through a renewal process.... Sustainable effective leadership occurs only when the experiences of sacrifice and stress of leadership are interchanged with those of renewal... unless a leader moves in and out of renewal he or she will not be able to sustain it.
Boyatsiz and McKee (2005)

The renewal cycle

Stop again, just for a moment and look at the model of the renewal cycle (Figure 1.2).
Ask yourself:

- What does renewal mean to me?
- Do I have a renewal process?
- What would an effective renewal process look like for me?

Figure 1.2: The renewal cycle

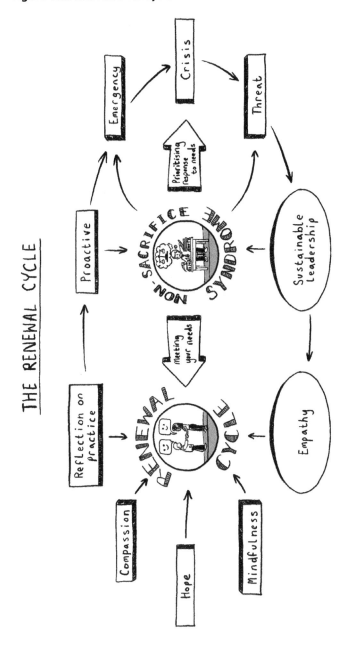

This model suggests that renewal involves pressing the pause button, and allowing yourself to be nurtured from the inside out. Mindfulness, hope and compassion are qualities that are nurtured first from within. They are then given expression in how we chose to care for ourselves and, subsequently, in the relationships we develop with others. As the model suggests, the impact is seen in the development of new ways of being, which in turn lead to the implementation of more effective leadership practices.

In Chapters 6 and 7, I talk more closely about the coaching relationship and how it can support the renewal cycle for school leaders. For now, however, I want to talk in greater detail about empathy and, more specifically, empathic listening.

Empathic listening

To relieve the burden of school leadership, school leaders need to be fully accepted for who they are (warts and all). This is what empathic listening facilitates. It allows a person to be listened to with 'unconditional positive regard.' This psychological term relates to the ability to suspend judgement, to listen in such a way that the person knows their own self-worth is not dependent on anything that they say or do.

Empathic listening is powerful because when listened to in this way, the person feels a great sense of liberation. The act of being listened to deeply helps them to listen to and understand themselves with a greater degree of accuracy. Thoughts, feelings and emotions that may have been weighing them down are released. Individuals are able to experience a lighter emotional and mental state.

The relationship between thoughts and feelings

Our thoughts influence how we feel and our feelings affect how we behave. It is only when we are listened to empathically that we are able to unpick how one affects the other. We make links between feelings and thoughts all the time in our daily lives. As a school leader, you do this constantly and probably do not realise the impact that the inter-relationship has on your levels of confidence and performance in the role.

For example, you feel miserable when you think about the school governor who constantly attempts to override your decisions; or you feel angry when you think about the member of staff who never has a good word to say about anything (particularly about you!); or you feel apprehensive when you think about a meeting that went wrong, knowing you don't want the same thing to happen the next time around.

All of these are natural emotions. The danger that many school leaders fall victim to is that, left unprocessed, these emotions cause an internal blockage, so the ability to lead oneself with integrity becomes severely limited. These people may find themselves in situations where they begin to lose confidence. As a result they act in ways which, far from increasing their self-confidence, actually diminish it. They adopt behaviours that do not match the image of the leader they really want to be. When they catch themselves behaving 'out of character', they may feel a mixture of shame, embarrassment, frustration, hurt and anger – emotions which, left unprocessed, decrease their ability to lead themselves and others with confidence and authenticity.

Through empathic listening, blockages are cleared, allowing the person to become more in tune with their own emotions; to learn not to run away from them, but to listen and understand them, and thus develop greater self-awareness and understanding. There is an increase in alignment between inner and outer worlds. Energy is not wasted in doing battle with negative internal emotions; energies are directed into developing behaviours that are congruent with the vision they truly wish to develop.

Making the crooked straight

Empathic listening also helps the individual to recognise and change their faulty thought processes, referred to by Butler and Hope as 'crooked thinking' (2005).

Have a look at the list below and see if any of these faulty thought processes are familiar to you:

Catastrophising
Predicting the worst outcome. If something goes wrong it will be a complete disaster. *'If I make a mistake that will be the end for me.'*

Overgeneralising
Assuming that because something happened once, it will always happen. *'They always forget to do the things I ask.'*

Exaggerating
Giving negative events more importance than they deserve and giving positive events less importance. *'This letter of complaint from Mr Jones means all parents are going to start complaining.'*

Discounting the positive
Rejecting good things as if they did not count (or using a negative filter). *'When they said that, they didn't really mean it. After all I know that I'm not really any good at writing reports.'*

Mind reading
Believing that you know what others are thinking. *'They know I've made a mess of this. They all think that I am incompetent.'*

Black-and-white thinking
Switching from one extreme to another. *'If I can't get this right, I might as well give up altogether.'*

Taking things personally

When someone asks you to do something differently, for example. *'You're criticising me.'*

Emotional reasoning:

Mistaking feelings for facts. *'I'm so worried; I know something is going to go wrong.'*

These faulty ways of thinking can severely limit someone's potential for dealing with the emotional demands of school leadership. Faulty inner dialogue hampers our ability to think clearly and to search for healthy ways for our emotional needs to be met. However, when we are listened to empathically, we are supported to adopt a different point of view. We are helped to think differently and – as a result – to feel differently. Therefore, empathic listening becomes the prime vehicle through which your emotional needs can be met. It becomes the means through which you:

- Come to know and trust yourself.
- Clarify your thinking and adopt new ways of being.
- Find the courage to learn how to change and grow.
- Discover meaning from your own life experiences.
- Build bonds of trust in your relationships with others.
- See the legitimacy of your own feelings validated through the empathic response of another.
- Learn how to take care of and nurture yourself.

When we are listened to empathically, we are given a gift; a gift that enriches our experience of what it means to be human. We discover that empathy is about being able to enter:

The private perceptual world of the other [...] means being sensitive moment by moment, to the changing felt meanings which flow in this other person, to the fear, rage or tenderness or whatever he or she is experiencing. It means temporarily living in the other's life, moving about in it

delicately without making judgements [...] Being empathetic is complex, demanding and strong – yet also a subtle and gentle way of being.
Rogers (1975) quoted in Pask and Joy (2007)

For a school leader, empathy may be the best remedy for healing the pain of your unmet emotional needs. It reminds you that, amidst the chaos of school life, you are worthy, you are valuable, and your story has the right to be listened to.

STOP, PAUSE AND REFLECT

Summary points:

- When emotional needs are met, healthy behaviour follows.
- The Sacrifice Syndrome is a symptom of leadership stress, the signs of which are prevalent in all senior leadership roles.
- We all have a need to feel valued, listened to and understood. Empathic listening is essential for meeting the core emotional needs of school leaders.

EXERCISE

How well are your emotional needs being met as a school leader?

Using a scale of 1–10, where 1 is low and 10 is high, reflect on the list below and give each need a score in relation to how well you think the need is being met for you.

Accepted	Forgiving	Private
Acknowledged	Free	Productive
Admired	Fulfilled	Reassured
Appreciated	Heard	Recognised
Approved of	Helped	Respected
Believed in	Helpful	Safe/secure
Capable	Important	Supported
Cared about	In control	Treated fairly
Challenged	Included	Trusted
Clear (not	Listened to	Understanding
confused)	Loved	Understood
Competent	Needed	Useful
Confident	Noticed	Valued
Forgiven	Powerful	Worthy

What does your scoring reveal to you?

What are the actions that you can take to ensure your emotional needs are being met in a balanced way?

CHAPTER 2:
Overcoming Loneliness at the Top

Loneliness is proof that your innate search for connection is intact.
Martha Beck
(American sociologist and author)

Overcoming Loneliness at the Top

In this chapter you will discover:
- Why change can be such an isolating process for school leaders.
- The four key reasons why power isolates.
- Why some types of support increase the isolation of school leaders.

Excessive anxiety and rumination, however, can be debilitating [...] and be exacerbated by feelings of isolation and loneliness associated with being 'at the top'.
Harris (2007)

When you become a school leader, understanding what the role is really asking of you can be hard work. Writing your application and getting through the interview is only a fraction of the process. The real work begins when you are in the post. This is when you come to fully understand what it means to be told 'the buck stops with you'; this is when you understand that you alone are responsible for everything that happens under your watch – good and bad.

The psychological adjustments that need to be made in order for you to fully accept and understand this can be like learning to walk again. Just as when you were a child learning to walk, you had to be supported by your loved ones to move from a place of unconscious incompetence to unconscious competence (Maslow's Four Stages of Learning, as shown in Figure 2.1), as a school leader you have to be supported to move to this confident place of being.

Without support, the experience for a school leader growing into their role can be both lonely and limiting. Progress can be slow and, in extreme cases, stunted; neither the leader nor those they lead seem able to reach the level of maturity necessary for sustained personal effectiveness.

Figure 2.1: Maslow's four stages of learning

No matter how well concealed it might be, every school leader's journey begins at the point of unconscious incompetence; it is only with time, patience, understanding and an environment that facilitates personal growth, that he or she can reach the point of unconscious competence. Take Ben's story as an example.

CASE STUDY—How a newly appointed deputy learnt to become a confident school leader

Ben was a newly appointed deputy Headteacher when we first began working together. At the beginning of the coaching relationship, four years previously, Ben had been somewhere between the unconscious and conscious incompetence stage. New in post, in a new school, in a new borough, with new relationships to form, he had to discover what it meant for him to make the role his own, and for him to feel both confident and comfortable as a new deputy Headteacher.

To begin with this was not an easy process; in order for him to move to a place of conscious competence – and eventually unconscious competence – we had to address his fears and insecurities (places that normally none of us like to go!) Like most of us when we venture into new arenas, Ben had his own set of worries and concerns about his new post. 'To begin with I felt very insecure. I kept thinking, am I the right person to do this job? Am I good enough to do it?'

Very often when we are new in post, the so-called 'imposter syndrome' looms large! Often it is typified by the thoughts Ben displayed, adopting false beliefs that we are frauds and will be found out sooner or later. Left unchallenged, these negative thoughts serve to fuel negative emotions and behaviours, often prolonging the time spent at the lower ends of Maslow's stages of learning.

In the early days of Ben's post, symptoms of the 'imposter syndrome' showed up as insecure behaviours. *'When I look back, it is true to say that because I felt so insecure, I lacked confidence. There was a lack of willingness to take risks, a lack of decisiveness and I was cautious rather than confident.'*

The provision of a confidential and trusted space allowed Ben to:
· Tell his leadership story and identify the key learning.

- Be honest about limiting behaviours that he wanted to let go of.
- Identify new behaviours that he wanted to develop.
- Surface his emotions and understand what they were telling him.
- Develop new ways of thinking.

This meant he was able to move to a much healthier and happier place as a leader. Now he is at the other end of Maslow's stages of learning – a leader who is unconsciously competent.

Ben reflected: *'Coaching has helped me to grow into the role and overcome past behaviours that would have held me back. When I started coaching, I focused largely on the negative. I am naturally someone who is quite cynical. Coaching has helped me to stop doing that. Coaching has helped me to get clarity around my own inner dialogue. When compared to the person I was before, I am now different. The whole process has enabled me to see growth in myself.'*

Power and loneliness at the top

Like all top leadership positions, school leadership – and headship in particular – brings with it the type of power that isolates: this is positional power. The higher up someone is in an organisation, the greater positional power brings increased pressures and responsibilities, as well as increased distance in relationships. Learning how to balance the need for human connection with the need to maintain the integrity of the leadership role is a challenge many school leaders face. They need to decide where their personal and professional boundaries lie, and the degree to which they will give of themselves.

When you are 'lower down' the school hierarchy, it is much easier to build relationships with those who are like you and to share problems with those who have had similar experiences. To begin with, there are more of you. If, for example, you are a class teacher in a primary school or a head of house in a secondary school, there will be others that hold the same position to whom you can turn for support. However, as you climb the hierarchy, the number of people holding the same or similar posts diminishes until, finally, you reach the top – Headteacher. You look around to find that there is no one in your setting who holds the same position as you.

In learning to cope with the isolation brought about by positional power, school leaders have to learn how to develop new relationships with themselves. Once the boundaries have been drawn, they need to learn how to be comfortable with their own company, and how to trust their own inner voice, particularly at times when no outside counsel is available.

Challenges to overcoming isolation at the top

During my work, I have identified four particular challenges that senior school leaders grapple with when seeking to find solutions for overcoming the feelings of isolation and loneliness that are a direct result of positional power:

- The myth of the super-head.
- Hidden expectations.
- Living under the leadership spotlight.
- Managing stereotype threat.

The myth of the super-head

People who champion the underdog, who stand up for what they believe in, whose social commentary challenges the status quo, appeal to me! In my late teens and early twenties I spent a great deal of my time listening to the music of the recently deceased American soul and jazz poet, Gill Scott Heron. In his commentary on the Cuban missile crisis, he penned the sardonic lines: *'There ain't no such thing as a Superman'*. And he is right! Superman (or Superwoman for that matter) does not exist! In the messiness and confusion of our everyday lives, we might all wish for some superhero to come and save the day, but life just isn't like that. It is down to us, mere mortals, to find the strength within ourselves, to become the heroes of our own stories.

But alas, education today has become dominated by the myth of the superhero, in the form of the 'super-head'. We have all been told how these super-heads have 'supernatural' powers to turn around failing schools. What the general public and media have yet to realise is that:

Leadership is not the private reserve of a few charismatic men and women. It is a process that ordinary people use when they are bringing forth the best in themselves and others.
Harris (2007)

The perpetuation of the super-head myth by the media only leads to greater fragility and isolation in the system. When super-heads fail, their descent becomes all too public. No one condones wrong-doing, but the current vogue for naming and shaming is both ruthless and heartless. Bill Gates illustrated this inequity perfectly when he said:

Developing a systematic way to help teachers get better is the most powerful idea in education today. The surest way to weaken it is to twist it into a capricious exercise in public naming and shaming. Let's focus on creating a personnel system that truly helps teachers improve.
Bill Gates (2012)

In this current climate, the struggle for many school leaders is how to determine the depth and integrity of their positional power. They must do this to counteract external voices and pressures (as discussed in Chapter 1) that diminish their own sense of value and self-worth. Behaviours and actions must be aligned with the qualities of true mortal heroes and not super men and women. Quite simply, it is:

... time to end the myth of the complete leader; the flawless being at the top, who's got it all figured out.
Harvard Business Review (2007)

In today's world of increasingly complex problems, no human being can meet this standard. Leaders who try only exhaust themselves, endangering their organisations in the process.

We are all human and, in my opinion, the best school leaders are the ones who have the courage to face their humanity head on; those who have the courage to admit their weaknesses and vulnerabilities and, in so doing, develop the personal wisdom and strength that leads to greater levels of both public and private authenticity.

Hidden expectations

School leaders are appointed because at interview they meet the explicit expectations of the interview panel. However, because the expectations are explicit and everyone understands what they are, the school leader is aware of the stresses that relate to the fulfilment of the statutory requirements of the role.

Hidden expectations are an entirely different matter. One of the greatest ones faced by school leaders (and specifically, Headteachers) is that they will be bulletproof (Figure 2.2). They are not meant to live their own lives or carry out their roles as living, breathing human beings who have feelings and emotions like everyone else. Instead they are meant to stand in the line of fire and say at the end of every day: *'I wasn't hurt.'*

Figure 2.2: Super-head armour

SUPER-HEAD ARMOUR*

BUT IN REALITY!

Absorbs criticism and complaints with ease!

*Doesn't exist.

This hidden expectation means that many school leaders do not seek out ways of addressing the internal pain that arises from routinely being in the line of fire; and just because an expectation is hidden, does not mean one should hide the negative impact from oneself.

When someone adopts what I call 'emotional lockdown' as a coping strategy, they not only lose some of their own personal power and authority, but they also weaken their ability to identify and respond to the hidden expectations of their role.

A leader who is not in tune with his or her own emotions is, by default, a leader who is not in tune with those they lead and manage. Leadership of others requires human, emotional connection on every level. Yes, there is a need for boundaries, but there is also a need for healthy, honest human relationships. Where these relationships exist, mutual respect, trust and understanding develop, and help to alleviate feelings of isolation.

Living under the leadership spotlight

Rarely a day goes by without there being a news story about education in the local or national press. For today's school leaders, the stakes are very, very high. It can seem that every action, whether individual or collective, is now under close public scrutiny. This can create battle fatigue, a feeling that the individual or the profession is always under attack.

The power that has been afforded to you by your status, particularly if you are a Headteacher, also means that you have to develop your 'political awareness' – a mental acuity necessary for navigating the often conflicting political agendas that now come your way.

Managing stereotype threat

Have you ever walked into a room and felt like you didn't belong, or felt that you were in the minority because of something to do with the very nature of who you are as a person – your gender, race, sexuality, age or religion? Can you recall how you felt? Can you remember the thoughts that rushed through your mind and how those thoughts impacted on your level of engagement with those in the room?

I can, and I'm sure if you think long and hard enough you will be able to think of examples from your own life.

CASE STUDY—My Story

My family are from Jamaica. In the late 1990s I became a Headteacher at 31, which was regarded at the time as a relatively young age. In those days, there were a few black Headteachers in my local authority – but I was the youngest.

Having been brought up in the inner-city and having experienced varying degrees of prejudice throughout my life, I was acutely aware of the racial stereotypes that had shaped my experience of being a black woman. When I stepped into the headship role, I suddenly found that I had to disprove the negative stereotypes about black women once again. Not only was this very painful, but at times – both psychologically and emotionally – it was a very lonely place to be.

The school advisors, governors and so on were not equipped either to understand or provide the emotional and psychological support that I needed to help me understand how my own background, culture and identity had shaped my experiences of becoming a school leader, as well as other people's responses to me in that role. Both formally and informally, I was told that people were there to support me, however they, or others who passed my way in the form of school support, were ill equipped to help me understand the complex interplay between my own self-image and other people's perceptions of me.

On more than one occasion, there were visitors to my school whose responses made it clear they had not expected to see a young black woman as the Headteacher of the school. Outwardly, I always sought to remain composed, calm and in control. On the inside, I felt enraged, upset and full of self-doubt – often all at the same time!

What I have described is what American social psychologist Claude M. Steele calls a 'stereotype threat'. He argues that whether we are conscious of it or not, many of us experience such a threat within our daily lives, this has a detrimental impact on our psychological and emotional well-being. He describes stereotype threat as:

Whenever we are in a situation where a bad stereotype about one of our identities could be applied, we know it. We know what 'people could think'. We know that anything that we do that fits the stereotype could be taken to confirm it. And we know that for that reason, we could be judged and treated accordingly.
Steele (2001)

In our attempt to overcome our hidden inner distress, we inadvertently subject ourselves to further psychological and emotional stress, as we battle to prevent our damaged emotions from erupting to the surface.

We are who we are. Headteachers and school leaders come in all shapes and sizes. But if Headteachers in particular are to be supported in overcoming the sense of isolation that the role brings (which can be crippling), then they need access to support that helps them overcome the often-overlooked and misunderstood impact of stereotype threat.

Why some types of support increase the feeling of isolation at the top

What is your definition of support? For me, support is about helping another person to carry a load. It's about providing non-judgemental advice and assistance to enable a group or individual to make sense for themselves on how best to carry the 'weight' they bear. For such support between individuals to be effective, there has to be mutual trust and respect on both sides; in the life of a school leader, a relationship of this kind is crucial.

Low trust/high accountability relationships

Trust is the glue of all our relationships. Day after day, we see the impact that trust has in our children's engagement with one another, with their teachers and with other key adults in their lives. When trust is high, individuals feel able to take risks and to be free to be who they are. They know they will not be judged for mistakes they make, and that any errors they make will be seen as opportunities for their growth and development.

For many school leaders, this is not the day-to-day reality. When trust is low and accountability is high, the person's thoughts, feelings and behaviours are about self-preservation. When we find ourselves in such relationships we feel worried, nervous and vulnerable. To protect ourselves, we place a barrier between ourselves and others. This means that the relationship only ever exists at a very superficial level. This can be damaging for anyone in need of support; the effort needed to keep the barrier up consumes both emotional and mental energy.

In a low trust/high accountability relationship (Figure 2.3), a disempowering dynamic exists that too often results in negative and non-aligned outcomes for that person. Because they have been told what to do, their actions are less rooted in who they are and little meaning is attached to the outcomes. As a result, he or she derives little ownership or satisfaction from their role.

Figure 2.3: Low trust/high accountability relationships

High trust/high accountability relationships

In contrast, coaching is a relationship that is marked by high levels of both trust and accountability. Because the accountability is to oneself, the potential that the relationship has for enabling someone to achieve their goals is far greater than one that is based on low trust/high accountability.

In a high trust/high accountability relationship (Figure 2.4) there are no walls or barriers. The person is free to be his or her self. It can be a place of great liberation. Energy is not exhausted in trying to protect a wounded and bruised self; rather that energy is used to heal and restore, and to bring the person back to a healthy state of being.

Figure 2.4: High trust/high accountability relationships

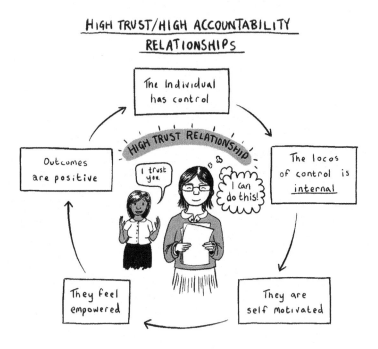

In a high trust/high accountability relationship, an empowering dynamic exists whereby the results are often the direct opposite of the demand-and-control type of 'support' that is all too often in evidence within the current education system.

Accountability is here to stay, but ...

The context for school leaders will always be one of high accountability. This is accentuated if you are the leader of an inner-city school where both the challenge to succeed and the stress levels are high. As a leader in an inner-city school, you not only have to be an expert leader and teacher, you also need to acquire emotional skill-sets that are more akin to those associated with social workers and counsellors.

Therefore, it stands to reason that to maintain optimum performance, school leaders – particularly those in inner-city schools – need relationships that are grounded in high levels of trust. When school leaders receive support that is based on an 'anything is possible' model of human potential, their opportunities for growth (and hence for their schools) is limitless. They are more likely to:

... take risks, be collaborative, deal with all issues, especially human process ones, in an open way and solve their problems.
Cockman *et al.* (2003)

STOP, PAUSE AND REFLECT

Summary points:

- The transition from unconscious incompetence to unconscious competence has to be a process that is fully supported.
- School leaders need personalised support to meet the challenges of school leadership.
- High trust/high (personal) accountability relationships help school leaders alleviate the feelings of isolation that arise from being at the top.

EXERCISE

Reflect for a moment on the professional relationships that you have in your life as a school leader, for example with governors, teachers, other members of your senior leadership team and school-improvement advisors. List them here:

_____

_____

_____

_____

_____

_____

Which of the four conditions below best matches each of these relationships?

1. HIGH accountability with LOW trust
The hallmarks of this type of relationship are:

- Fear
- Mistrust
- Resentment

Leading to:

- Restricted personal performance
- Short-term impact on standards
- Unsustainable results

2. HIGH accountability with HIGH trust
The hallmarks of this type of relationship are:

- Openness
- Cooperation

- Understanding
- Empathy

Leading to:

- High personal performance
- Long-term impact on standards
- Sustainable results

3. LOW accountability with LOW trust

The hallmarks of this type of relationship are:

- Complacency
- Smugness
- Arrogance

Leading to:

- Compromised personal performance
- Negative impact on standards
- Poor results

4. LOW accountability with HIGH trust

The hallmarks of this type of relationship are:

- Self-motivation
- Self-doubt
- Self-reliance

Leading to:

- Confusion around expected personal performance standards
- Minimal impact on standards
- Erratic results

What impact are these relationships having on how you feel about your role as a school leader?

CHAPTER 3:
Understanding Self

*Knowing others
is intelligence
Knowing yourself
is true wisdom
Mastering others
is strength
Mastering yourself
is true power.*

**Lao Tzu
(Ancient Chinese philosopher and poet)**

Understanding Self

In this chapter you will discover:
- How to answer four essential questions that will help you to deepen your understanding of who you are.
- How to begin living a more conscious life as a school leader.
- What aspects of yourself need to change to enable you to lead in alignment with who you really are.

Leaders often do not fully recognise the extent to which, 'who they are' affects virtually every aspect of their organisation.
Branden (1994)

Understanding who we are and what makes us tick has been the domain of psychologists since the 1930s. We all want to know the extent to which nature and nurture combine to give us our own distinctive characteristics. Why do we respond to certain situations in the way we do? Why do some scenarios elicit a calm response from one person, yet induce feelings of terror and fear in another? Why is it that some people are headstrong and independent, while others are less so? Why is it that some thrive in the company of many, while others prefer the company of a few?

There is a need for school leaders to fully understand who they are, so that they can be centred within themselves and lead from a position of deep inner connectedness and self-trust.

Who are you?

The question *'Who are you?'* is simple enough to ask, but far more complex to answer. As a coach, I believe there are four key questions that school leaders need to ask of themselves if they are to gain a better understanding of who they are and what the experience of being a school leader means to them:

- What do I think is true about myself?
- What do I think is important in life?
- How do I respond to what I think is important?
- How much do I value myself?

As you answer each question, you will gain another level of understanding about yourself, until you can say with confidence: *'Now I know who I am, why I behave as I do, and what I intend to do about it'.*

When we understand ourselves better, we are able to live our lives more consciously, and in doing so exhibit greater control over life's events instead of feeling that life is controlling us.

The answer to each question provides us with answers to four key areas of our inner life.

- Beliefs
- Values
- Mindset
- Self-esteem

All of the areas above interact with one another, and the relationship between them impacts upon 'who we are'.

- Your beliefs determine, often at a subconscious level, the choices you have made.
- Your values determine the actions you take.
- Your mindset determines the attitude with which you approach life.
- Your self-esteem determines how you treat yourself and how others treat you.

In the life of a school leader, we tend to think that the stress of the role comes purely from external sources. However, a mind that does not know itself cannot operate at a higher level of consciousness; as a result, subconscious self -limiting habits and ways of being can cause as much stress to a school leader's working life as external sources. We need to know who we are in order to live our lives more fully and lead with a greater degree of confidence. When we are able to do so we:

- Feel empowered.
- Become better communicators and listeners.
- Are able to deal much more effectively with conflict.
- Understand how we can positively influence others.
- Know what it takes to develop successful relationships.

Making sense of who you are as a leader

As you read through the rest of this chapter, I'd like to invite you to think about your responses to each of the four questions mentioned earlier. These were:

- What do I think is true about myself?
- What do I think is important in life?
- How do I respond to what I think is important?
- How much do I value myself?

In seeking to find answers, think about your formative years. Think about those who had the greatest influence upon you and how they shaped your thinking about life and the person you are today. Think about the key events in your life and the meaning you derived from them. Think about the choices you have made and how they have influenced the life that you lead as a school leader.

Question 1: What do you think is true is about yourself? (Exploring beliefs)

Your answer to this question can uncover much that you may have been previously unaware of about yourself. When we ask ourselves:

'What do I think is true about myself?' we are uncovering our beliefs about our own personal identities. These beliefs may not exist in our minds as explicit propositions. They may be so implicit in our thinking that we are hardly aware of them at all; yet they clearly lie behind our actions.
Branden (1994)

Our beliefs are assumed truths. They are our inner statements about ourselves in which we are emotionally invested. They have shaped us and (probably, without us even realising it) have been with us since childhood, picked up from those who possessed the greatest influence over us during our formative years. Our beliefs are like a hidden undercurrent that has influenced who we are today.

The longer you occupy a school leadership position, with the variety of experiences and challenges that the role brings, the more your beliefs are tested. There will be times when it may be necessary for you to throw away your beliefs and create new ones, but this takes a great deal of self-awareness and is rarely achieved alone.

Self-limiting beliefs
Self-limiting beliefs (Figure 3.1) are the ones which have the greatest potential to impact negatively upon achieving one's full potential. We develop self-limiting beliefs to protect us from future pain. Usually they develop (during our formative years) in response to painful experiences. From these experiences we create our own, often skewed, generalisations about life.

These generalisations become deeply embedded in our subconscious and then manifest themselves as self-limiting beliefs that influence much of what we think, say and do.

Figure 3.1: Self-limiting beliefs

Example of limiting beliefs

- I am powerless.
- Nothing I say is worth being listened to.
- Everything I do has to be perfect.
- I am worthless.
- I can't handle conflict.

Limiting behaviours dictated by the belief

- Not standing up for your self.
- Not speaking up.
- Becoming risk averse.

- Acting defensively.
- Giving into others.

When we allow our lives to be shaped by these self-limiting beliefs, the behaviours we adopt reinforce our own beliefs and we become expert in creating our own self-fulfilling prophecies.

Self-limiting beliefs in action

Observe 'challenging' children in your school and you will see exactly how a self-limiting belief can become a self-fulfilling prophecy. If these children have an underlying limiting belief that they are worthless, they will adopt negative behaviours that cause them to be chastised by others. The responses they receive from others serve only to fuel their belief that they are worthless and so, in their minds, the belief is proved right and they continue perpetuating a vicious cycle of negative thoughts, beliefs and behaviours. That is, until – hopefully – a time arrives whereby the school's behaviour policy or PSHE (Personal, Social, Health Education) curriculum, causes them to believe something different about themselves; as a result they begin to adopt new positive behaviours that in turn create a more positive picture of reality for them.

It is often the same with adults. We remain oblivious to the impact of our self-limiting beliefs until circumstances, or another person, causes us to reframe what we think and to ask ourselves: *'Is that really true? On what past experience have I based this belief, and what impact has holding onto this belief had on my life?'*

Reflect for a moment or two on some of the self-limiting beliefs listed earlier.

- Do any of these resonate with you?
- Can you identify where they might have come from?
- What are the behaviours that you have adopted that may have reinforced these beliefs?

- How have these behaviours impacted on the way in which you see yourself?
- What beliefs need to replace your self-limiting beliefs?
- What new behaviours do you need to adopt to enable your new beliefs to impact more positively on your life?

Question 2: What do you think is important in life? (Exploring values)

Our values stem from our beliefs and, in the same way as we acquire our beliefs, they are developed over time from our family, friends, culture and those close to us. And again, like our beliefs, they contribute to our sense of who we are. They are our internal moral compass and they determine the direction that our lives take. When we act in alignment with our values, we have a very strong sense of self. We see ourselves as being true to who we are. If you want to excel as a leader, you have to know what motivates you; what inspires you; where your inner fuel comes from. You have to know what your values are and how they influence your choices, your behaviours and the way in which you are seen by others.

In thinking about values, it can be helpful to think of them as roots that hold your personal vision in place. Like the roots of a tree (Figure 3.2), our values lie deep beneath the surface. When we look at a tree, we look at its height, the breadth of its trunk and the quality of its fruit, knowing that the quality of the fruit is dependent on the integrity of its roots.

Figure 3.2: Values tree

It is the same for school leaders. When you are a school leader, other people assess your integrity – the true meaning of your values – by your words and your actions. When there is inner and outer alignment, you are seen as authentic and true.

Below is a list of commonly held values. If you feel that any values you hold dear are missing, add them to the list. Reflect on the list and try to select your top ten.

Commonly held values

Achievement	Humour	Resourcefulness
Balance (home and work)	Independence	Respect
	Integrity	Team work
Courage	Kindness	Tolerance
Creativity	Listening	Trust
Equality	Making a	Truthfulness
Excellence	difference	Vitality
Family	Patience	
Generosity	Personal growth	
Honesty	Reliability	

Once you have selected your top ten, try and identify your top *three* – the three that others would say you lived your life by. These won't be values others recognise because every day you wear a T-shirt saying: *'These are my top three values'*; they will be recognised because your actions testify to your true nature.

After you have identified your top three, ask yourself: *'What are the behaviours that I need to adopt each and every day that demonstrate to myself and others that these values are central to who I am as a person?'*

Question 3: How do you respond to what you think is important? (Exploring mindsets)

Part of your ability to live in true alignment with yourself will depend to a great extent on your mindset – that is, what you think and believe about yourself and your own perceived abilities as a leader.

When you enter a mindset, you enter a new world. In one world-the world of fixed traits – success is about proving you're smart or talented. Validating yourself. In the other – the world of changing qualities – it's about stretching yourself to learn something new. Developing yourself.
Dweck (2012)

In her bestselling book *Mindsets*, Professor Carol Dweck argues that there are two key kinds of mindsets that people can have: a fixed mindset or a growth mindset.

Key characteristics of mindsets (adapted from Dweck, 2012)

Fixed mindset

- Personal qualities and attributes carved in stone.
- Pressure to prove oneself.

- A need to always be right/correct.
- Mistakes are a character fault and a sign of weakness.

Growth mindset

- Personal qualities can be nurtured and developed.
- Delight in personal growth and development.
- At ease with new situations; no need to 'shout the loudest'.
- Mistakes are fertile ground for self-learning and development.

Dweck argues that these two quite distinct mindsets profoundly affect the way we live our lives. Reflect on yourself for a moment.

- Which mindset do you veer towards the most?
- What impact does your predominating mindset have on the way you approach life's challenges?
- What impact does your predominating mindset have on how you see yourself?

These are important questions to consider, particularly if you recognise that you veer more towards a fixed mindset.

The limitations of a fixed mindset
As Dweck points out, people 'with a fixed mindset do not admit and correct their deficiencies'. There may be a number of reasons for this:

- Fear of being judged.
- Lack of self-awareness.
- Low self-esteem.

When we talk about leadership in schools and adults working with children, the fixed mindset is one that cannot be left unaddressed, because it limits not only yourself, but also your school.

A fixed mindset means you become risk averse for fear of being proved wrong. Your creativity and ability to think 'outside the box' can be severely limited, because you rely more heavily on the left frontal part of your brain (the rational, logical, reasoning part) to carry out the leadership functions of your role. To be fully effective as a school leader, you need to be able to draw upon the capacities of the right frontal parts of your brain, so that you can also be creative and intuitive in your approach to problem-solving and finding solutions.

Leading with a fixed mindset is professionally limiting. It is a leadership style that seeks to meet the ego's unmet, childlike needs for immediate gratification and affirmation, and it is often uncritical and unquestioning. It is a style of leadership that lacks the maturity to be able to take criticism without seeing it as a personal affront. When a person's self-awareness is low and they do not seek counsel or support from others (because they see no need to), outcomes are usually less than satisfactory.

When bosses become controlling and abusive, they put everyone into a fixed mindset. This means instead of learning, growing and moving the company forward, everyone starts worrying about being judged. It starts with the bosses worrying about being judged, but it winds up being everybody's fear about being judged. It's hard for courage and innovation to survive a companywide fixed mindset.
Dweck (2012)

Faced with the vehement implementation of new OFSTED inspection criteria, it is easy to understand why a climate of fear exists in many schools. Understandably, school leaders are worried about the judgements that might be made about their leadership and their schools. This fear has led many school leaders, often unconsciously, to lead from a fixed mindset. However, this only serves to weaken their own ability – and consequently that of their staff – to rise to the very real challenges presented by an increasingly dehumanised inspection regime.

We all know that OFSTED is a reality and is more than likely here to stay! So you have to take charge; you have to be able to rise above the fear and adopt a mindset that will ultimately lead to greater self-knowledge and success for yourself as a school leader.

Developing a growth mindset

Hitch your wagon firmly to something larger than yourself.
Barack Obama (44th President of the United States)

Wise words, and, as a school leader, you have most definitely done that! What could be bigger than believing you can make a significant difference to the life chances of the children in your school? You know the future belongs to them, so your wagon is hitched to helping them develop the attitude, skills and mindsets that will enable them to seize it with both hands. When you have a big vision, it is imperative that you develop a mindset that will enable you to move beyond the limitations of what others might consider possible, and in doing so increase your capacity to think and achieve big.

Here is Dweck's description of people with a growth mindset:

They were self-effacing people who constantly asked questions and had the ability to confront the most brutal answers [...] that is the ability to look failure in the face, even their own, while maintaining faith that they would succeed in the end.
Dweck (2012)

As a school leader, when you are able to do this, you will be much better equipped at strengthening your own inner resolve and resilience. In doing so, you will also develop the inner tools that protect your own self-esteem and self-worth. You learn that in developing the ability to overcome setbacks, difficulties and self-doubt, you become much better at valuing yourself for who you are, and knowing that within each perceived failure lays an opportunity for greater self-growth and understanding.

Question 4: How much do you value yourself? Exploring self-esteem

Today's organisations need not only an unprecedented higher level of knowledge and skill amongst all those who participate, but also a higher level of independence, self-reliance, self-trust and the capacity to exercise initiative. In a word, self-esteem.
Branden (1994)

Self-esteem is the 'reputation we acquire with ourselves' as a direct result of living out our beliefs and values. A healthy self-esteem allows you to:

* Be comfortable with who you are and to be comfortable with others.
* Face challenges from a position of inner strength.
* Accept criticism and not see it as a personal attack.
* Embrace change and the ambiguities that often accompany it.
* Handle conflict with dignity.

N.B. Low self-esteem produces the opposite results.

In the context of schools, self-esteem is often a term we use when talking about the child who never looks at us in the eye when they are spoken to, or the child who constantly craves attention and consistently misbehaves. In these children we see how the human spirit manifests its need to be validated.

A healthy self-esteem is what we all need to survive and thrive. You, as a school leader, need it more than most! Every day you are faced with challenges to your self-esteem from both inside and outside the school gates, whether in the form of a complaint from an angry parent, or taking a failing member of staff through competency procedures. Issues of this type will always cause you to question who you are, what you believe in, and what you will stand up for.

Rarely in these situations are you dealing with people who share the same values and belief systems as yourself. Very often they are confused about their own esteem needs and how they want these needs to be met. They don't know what their esteem needs are and you – as a leader – have to become expert in recognising and understanding how to meet these needs.

When dealing with such scenarios as a school leader, it is essential that you have a healthy self-esteem. You have to be sure of who you are so that self-doubt is not allowed to take hold of your inner resolve and cause you to be someone other than your best self. On a good day, the roots of who you are will provide the support that you need to confidently face these challenges. However, when energy levels are low and stress levels are high, self-esteem takes a dip. It can be very difficult to lead others and rise above the challenges of school leadership when the roots of who you are have been neglected; just as the roots of a tree need regular watering to keep the tree upright and able to bear fruit, you need to pay regular attention to your own roots – your own values and beliefs – so that you can stand tall against the storms of school leadership.

Protecting and building you own self-esteem

Protecting and building your own self-esteem is about learning to be conscious of your thoughts, feelings and behaviours, so that you can make the right choices about the way in which you live your life. It is about moving from an 'unconscious life' (in which you are not fully awake to the consequences of your unexamined thoughts and actions) to living an examined life (in which you make conscious

choices regarding your thoughts, feelings and behaviour)
(Figure 3.3). Ultimately, this leads to a greater degree of inner
alignment and both personal and professional self-fulfilment.

**Figure 3.3: Unconscious and conscious living
(adapted from Jay (2009)**

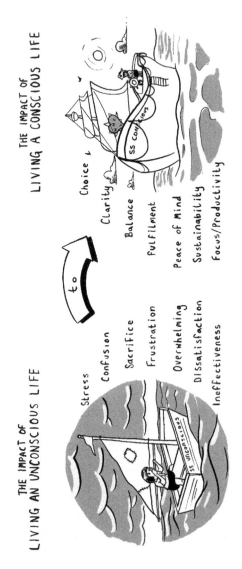

STOP, PAUSE AND REFLECT

Summary points:

- If we are to understand others, we first need to understand ourselves.
- Increased self-knowledge and understanding improves the way in which leaders lead themselves.
- Self-esteem is a by-product of the relationship between our values, our beliefs and our mindsets.

EXERCISE

How well do you know yourself?

Beliefs

- To what degree are you aware of the beliefs that you have picked up about yourself from your parents and others around you when you were growing up?
- To what degree have these beliefs served you, and how have they impacted on the choices that you have made?

Values

- As a school leader, what are the values that you believe to be of most importance to you?
- What behaviours do you adopt that show that you are living your life in alignment with these values?

Mindset

- Would you consider yourself to have a growth mindset or a fixed mindset?
- To what degree does your predominating mindset impact upon your performance as a school leader?

Self-esteem

- What was your self-esteem like as a child?
- How did your self-esteem develop as you grew older?
- On a day-to-day basis, are you aware of the factors that contribute to the growth of your self-esteem and the factors that inhibit it?

CHAPTER 4:
Learning to Drop the
Leadership Mask

You gain strength, courage and confidence by every experience in which you really stop to look fear in the face. You must do the thing which you think you cannot do.

Eleanor Roosevelt
(American politician and First Lady)

Learning to Drop the Leadership Mask

In this chapter you will discover:
- The reasons leaders wear masks.
- The benefits of being able to drop the leadership mask.
- Why success is dependent upon our ability to ask for help.

All the world's a stage,
and all the men and women merely players:
They have their exits and their entrances;
and one man in his time plays many parts.
William Shakespeare (*As You Like It*)

The leadership mask

Masks are worn to conceal the true identity of the wearer. In theatre and ceremony they are explicit in both their form and function; in leadership, this is not so. As a school leader, the mask that you wear is far more subtle. It isn't made of clay, paper or wood. It doesn't have elaborate patterns or features painted across it. The mask that you wear is invisible, but it hides your inner world of thoughts, feelings and emotions.

The school leader's stage

In Simon Walker's book, *Leading Out of Who You Are: Discovering the Secret of Undefended Leadership*, he introduces the theory of 1960s psychologist Erving Goffman that equates human behaviour to that of living out one's life onstage. His theory proposes that, for all of our interactions, we are trying to manage the response that we get from our audience. The degree of intimacy and trust that exists between the performer and the audience will influence his or her performance on stage. Depending on the degree of intimacy and trust, the performer will adapt that performance for every situation, to try to get a favourable response from the audience.

Figure 4.1: Performing to different audiences

Goffman proposes that the routines people adopt and the feedback that they receive are all part of how they develop their sense of self-worth. These acts and routines are all performed on the person's front stage.

The front stage becomes the place where we perform for our audience; often more than one audience at a time [...] the front stage becomes our place for conviction and confidence.
Walker (2007)

In an education context, we can quite easily see how this theory relates to the life of school leaders. School leaders have multiple audiences to play to: governors, pupils, parents, teachers, inspectors and numerous other stakeholders (Figure 4.1). Depending on the different factors – that may be competing factors – these audiences can be friendly or hostile. Levels of intimacy and trust can sometimes be inspiringly high and at other times depressingly low. As a school leader, you know the reality of what it means to try to give an outstanding performance for each of these audiences on a daily basis. It is exhausting!

But you have to do it! And you have to be able to give the performance each audience expects. For this, you have to don your leadership mask because the mask protects your feelings. When the critics aren't as forthcoming in their praise for your performance as you had expected, your true feelings are kept hidden, so that you can still hold your head up high and walk back on stage for your next scheduled performance.

The show must go on ... says who?

As a young Headteacher, I honestly believed there was only one option open to me and that was to soldier on at all costs. I wasn't aware that there was another option – that was, to ask for help. Well, actually that's not quite right. My belief was, rightly or wrongly, that if I asked for help, it would either be seen as a sign of weakness or it would be used against me. I see many school leaders adopt this position in today's high stakes/high risks educational landscape. It is understandable.

Coming out from behind our defences

We all have defence mechanisms. Often, we are barely aware of them. They are the thought processes and behaviours that protect us from being hurt. They serve to keep us safe from situations or other people that we perceive will cause us harm. Most school leaders feel that every day they have to defend themselves against 'the slings and arrows of outrageous fortune'.

Left unchecked, defensive behaviours cause not only a distancing in relationships with others, but also a distancing in the relationship that the individual has with him or herself. They become a stranger, not only to work colleagues, but also to their loved ones. The person that they see reflected in the mirror is the one who is wearing the mask.

Many school leaders feel uncomfortable leading from this place. Deep inside, many of them know that their defensive behaviours lessen their ability to be true to themselves and their values. Their true nature is compromised, as well as their ability to lead with authenticity and purpose.

If I can't get upward feedback – what do I do?

If this is your reality, then a little bit of knowledge about a psychological tool called the Johari Window might just help (Figure 4.2). It may decrease any inner dissonance that you have about the way in which you are performing in your role.

Developed in the 1950s by two American psychologists, Joseph Luft and Harry Ingham, the Johari Window is a useful tool that can help you begin thinking about how you might lessen your defences and bring more of your true self into the open arena of school leadership.

Figure 4.2: The Johari Window

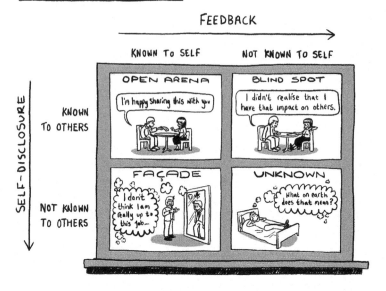

Within the Johari Window there are four areas:

1. The public arena
What is known by you about yourself and is also known by others. This is the area in which relationships develop and flourish. When there is open communication and no hiding behind masks or learnt defences, people create a space for interacting that invites openness, honesty and trust.

2. The blind spot
What is unknown by you about yourself, but which others see (through your body language, tone of voice, habits, mannerisms, etc.). For all of us, our blind spots can be our Achilles' heel. Very often, these are unconscious behaviours. If we never learn how to address our blind spots, we create a world in which relationships have the potential to become

fractured because we are unaware of how our behaviours can cause upset or pain to others.

3. The façade

What you know about yourself that others do not know (the feelings, prejudices and façade we put up). The façade is what you see or know about yourself that is deliberately hidden from others, often because there is a perceived need for self-protection. The problem here is that it takes time, energy and emotion to constantly hide behind a façade; doing so diverts key personal resources away from actually being and living as your true authentic self. In addition, those around you pick up that 'something isn't right'. They may not know exactly what it is you're 'hiding', but your behaviours give subtle, often subconscious, clues that you are not being your true self. Left unaddressed this can lead to loss of your self-confidence, and loss of confidence from others in your ability to lead.

4. The unknown

What is unknown to you about yourself and is also unknown by others. The unknown area is that part of you that is buried in your subconscious. If someone is in need of very deep emotional healing, their issues can be explored and discussed through work with expertly trained therapists or counsellors.

Unbiased processing

To move to a place in which leadership is less of a closed affair and more about the opening of self, each person needs to be supported in developing skills for what has been termed unbiased processing. Unbiased processing is about being both willing and able to work on all aspects of one's self:

It involves not denying, distorting, exaggerating or ignoring private knowledge, internal experiences and externally based evaluative information.
The Leadership Quarterly (2005)

It is a process that you can begin simply by being prepared to answer a few questions about the first three sections of the Johari Window.

Public arena

- How would you describe your public self?
- When you are at your best, what are the qualities that you are proud that others see in you?
- How does your public self impact upon the way in which you see yourself as a leader?
- To what degree is your public self aligned with your private self?

Blind spot

- Have you received any feedback that might be an indication of a limiting behaviour or habit?
- How have you responded?
- What difference would it make to your leadership if you could address this?
- If you have not received feedback, have you 'sensed' unease from others when you have behaved in a particular manner?

Façade

- Are there aspects of you as a leader that you are deliberately keeping from others?
- Who are the others that you are keeping this information from?
- What are your reasons for doing so?
- If addressed could this make a difference to the way in which you lead yourself and others?

Unknown
- Not going here!

Learning to ask for help

Vulnerability sounds like truth and feels like courage. Truth and courage aren't always comfortable, but they are never weaknesses.
Brown (2012)

With the proviso that mutual respect, trust and understanding exist between the parties involved (as detailed in Chapter 2), learning to ask for help is one of the greatest things a leader can do. By acknowledging this fact, they can accept and redefine their vulnerability.

Learning to ask for help is about modelling to yourself and future school leaders, that the role can be done, but in a more holistic and humane way. As I have mentioned elsewhere in this book, I have a dislike for the term 'super-head' because I feel it creates a false notion of what this role is about. To be a school leader, whether as a Headteacher or in another role, is to be human. Being human is about feeling; it is about connecting, learning to live with uncertainty, fear and self-doubt, being vulnerable to change and uncertainty. It is, to quote the title of Brené Brown's book, about *Daring Greatly* (Brown, 2012).

Being a school leader is about being willing to engage with the communities that you serve, while staying rooted in your values and your purpose, even when league tables and SATs results tell only one part of the story of your school's journey. To quote again from Brené Brown, it is about showing:

... courage beyond measure. It's daring greatly and after the result of doing greatly isn't a victory march, as it is a quiet sense of freedom, mixed with a little battle fatigue.
Brown (2012)

Coaching and learning to dare greatly

If we are to dare greatly, we have to take Goffman's theory a little further and be prepared to do some work backstage before each of our performances. Backstage, we can: STOP, PAUSE AND REFLECT. Backstage, we can drop our leadership mask and discover how to get back in touch with our true selves. We all have a backstage, which represents our inner world. In the life of school leaders seeking to be the best they can be, the backstage should be a safe and protected environment where, with a trusted confidante, they can:

- share their doubts and confusions
- share their defeats and upsets
- edit and re-write the script for their next performance
- rehearse their lines.

Figure 4.3: The backstage coach

The coach sits backstage, ready to lend a listening ear, ready to hear how your multiple performances have gone, ready to help you prepare for your next show (Figure 4.3).

Achieving both external and inner victories

When a school leader seeks to work on both their front of house and backstage performances, they increase their ability to be continually outstanding in front of all of their audiences. Moreover the term 'outstanding' ceases to become a narrow definition for defining public victories, such as SATs and GCSE results. It also becomes a term for defining their inner victories, marked by their growing self-awareness and ability to reflect, a trait that Daniel Goleman has identified in many outstanding leaders.

Perhaps the most telling (though less visible) sign of self-awareness is the propensity for self-reflection and thoughtfulness [...] Many outstanding leaders, in fact, bring to their work life the thoughtful mode of self-reflection.
Goleman (2003)

Case study: How a Headteacher learnt to drop the leadership mask

Siobhan entered my office looking tired, worn and exhausted. She later said: *'I was exhausted, physically, and mentally. I had begun to lose weight and that's always a sign for me that something is wrong.'*

Not really knowing what she was looking for, Siobhan came to see me simply because she knew that so far her experience of headship had not been what she had expected. Her hope was that coaching might help her find a new way to feel fulfilled again as a Headteacher.

During our work together, it became apparent that in seeking to cope with the stresses and demands of the role Siobhan had subconsciously adopted behaviours that had caused her to 'shrink into herself'. She recalls: *'I remember at our first session that I kept on saying "That's not me". Hearing myself out loud was a very important first step in reclaiming myself again. I had to explain and say out loud what I was feeling. It was scary, but it was a necessary step. I had to be honest with myself.'*

As Siobhan opened up about her own inner dialogue and accompanying behaviours, she came to the realisation that her 'leadership mask' had only served to diminish her view of herself as a leader, and had stopped her true self from taking centre stage.

She explained: *'As Headteacher I knew that I had to keep an eye on the future and plan ahead, but the day-to-day aspects took over and I wasn't able to look forward enough. The challenges that I had to face and the behaviours that I adopted meant that I felt unfulfilled and unhappy. I felt as if I had lost myself.'*

In order to help Siobhan find herself again, it was imperative that coaching provided her with a safe space, to allow her to drop her leadership mask. There, in the safety of my office, away from the pressures of school life, Siobhan and I met every half term. We explored:

- Her reasons for choosing to be a Headteacher.
- The challenges she had faced and what she had learnt about herself.
- The impact that certain challenging individuals where having upon her and how she could change her emotional responses.
- What it meant for her to be in control and how she could ensure that her locus of control was always internal and not overridden by external factors.
- Practical steps she could take to re-ignite her vision and her passion for the role she was in.

Before we finished our designated number of sessions, Siobhan had not only successfully led her school through an OFSTED inspection, but she also secured a new headship post. Remember, this was someone who prior to coaching was ready to throw in the towel!

In learning to drop the leadership mask, Siobhan recalled: *'There was a definite feeling of change. I could almost feel it physically. It felt exhilarating! The process reignited my passion. That part of me was stirred again.'*

Letting go

It is often in the act of asking for help and talking a problem through that people are able to work out how to let go of their problems. It's all too easy to become attached to them. We can find a distorted comfort in problems that have defined our experience of who we are, which is particularly true if a problem is typical of a group to which we belong. Shared problems can give us a collective identity, whereby the problem, although painful, is less of a threat when it feels that you are 'all in it together'. To ask for help and to find a way to cut ties with the problem, and any collective 'group think' that exists, may cause someone to question their identity and their place within the group. This can lead to a situation in which they, consciously or subconsciously, stop themselves from taking the action that will mark them out as being separate and different from their perceived peer group.

However, people in high-stress roles, such as that of school leader, have to find ways of abandoning the collective, limiting mindset of others, and ask for help. When someone makes a conscious decision to leave the collective mindset, they have taken the first essential step of learning to help themselves.

What prevents us from seeking help?

There is no strength in not asking for help. Very often, when school leaders don't seek help, they weaken their own self-image and what they can achieve. Nothing great is ever achieved alone. We all need the support of others to help us achieve our goals. There are many reasons why people don't ask for help. Most are rooted in the:

- Fear of being judged.
- Fear of being seen as weak or as a failure.
- Fear of not knowing the answers to problems that have arisen.
- Fear that the help that is asked for might not match one's needs.
- Fear of what other people will say or think.

When we ask for help, we bring to life the values of honesty, trust and respect. If we are going to develop emotional maturity within our schools, to deal effectively with the vulnerabilities of human nature, these values must be deeply embedded into our school support structures. This is partly what is needed if we are ever going to realise the dream of:

A personnel system that truly helps teachers to improve.
Bill Gates (2012)

In difficult times, we need to model to ourselves and others how the values of honesty, trust and respect are lived out and given meaning. When we turn to another person, asking for help, we see how these values bring hope, security and an inner determination that problems can be dealt with and overcome.

Why do athletes have coaches?

Athletes know that being their best requires them to get help to enable them to develop the physical, mental and emotional prowess needed to succeed. Take Jessica Ennis, Mo Farah, Bradley Wiggins and other great athletes; none would have achieved the levels of success they have done in their careers if they had not sought help. The help they received enabled them to get over knockbacks and defeats and come back stronger, more resilient and more focused. These days, it is common for athletes to have coaches, and to be very public about the fact as they acknowledge the debt that they owe to them. They publicly celebrate the fact that their professional achievements have been the result of a trusting and motivational partnership, where the focus is on fulfilling their potential.

Whatever our goals, whatever our ambitions, we need help, so that when the going gets tough – as it always does – we won't fall down, but will be supported with renewed focus and energy to carry on towards our dream. When we ask for help, we start on the path to finding a bigger picture of ourselves.

STOP, PAUSE AND REFLECT

Summary points:

- School leaders increase their levels of effectiveness when they learn how and when to drop their leadership mask.
- Left unchecked, defensive behaviours can lessen a school leader's ability to lead from a position of strength and authenticity.
- Learning to ask for help is not a sign of weakness – it is one of the most courageous things a school leader can do.

CHAPTER 5:
Moving Out of Comfort Zones

As you move outside of your comfort zone, what was once the unknown and frightening becomes your new normal.
**Robin Sharma
(Canadian leadership
expert, lawyer and writer)**

Moving Out of Comfort Zones

In this chapter you will discover:
- How your experience of the comfort zone has shaped who you are as a leader.
- The role your inner voice plays in influencing the extent of your own personal growth.
- The role that coaching can play in helping you step outside your comfort zone.

Life begins at the edge of your comfort zone.
Neil Donald Walsch (American author, actor, screenwriter and speaker)

Comfort zones are the areas of our lives in which we experience very little stress and in which we are able to operate with a degree of ease and familiarity. They exist on both personal and professional levels, and can be both positive and negative. On the positive side they can be affirming and provide us with a space in which we can fully exhibit our talents. On the negative side, when we are not conscious of changes within ourselves and our environment, they can severely limit our growth.

Positive and negative aspects of operating within our comfort zone

Positive aspects
These occur when we are operating at a level that we find both stimulating and rewarding, and stress is minimal or easily managed.

- A sense of security.
- A sense of safety.

- A feeling of being in control.
- A sense of confidence and well-being.
- Freedom and relaxation.

Negative aspects

These occur when we have outgrown our comfort zone, but have ignored internal or external signs that it is time for us to step out and move on.

- Limited growth.
- Stagnation.
- Missed opportunities.
- Decreased confidence.
- Fear.

First steps into the teacher comfort zone

Think back to when you first became a teacher, to your very first class, your very first parent's meeting, your very first assembly. No doubt you will remember those very first feelings of fear, anxiety and worry as you sought to get to grips with new experiences. Hopefully, you will also remember when those feelings began to subside and you were no longer as worried and fearful – when you began to operate effectively within your comfort zone. As you grew in confidence about your skills as a teacher, so too did your ability to manage your classroom, and your interactions with parents, peers and colleagues. Your comfort zone became a positive place for you to be (Figure 5.1). It became a place that:

- Confirmed your identity as a teacher.
- Affirmed your strengths, which boosted your levels of confidence and self-esteem.
- Nurtured belief in your own abilities and enabled you to experience the freedom to be creative and try out new ideas.
- Allowed you to trust in yourself.

Figure 5.1: The comfort zone

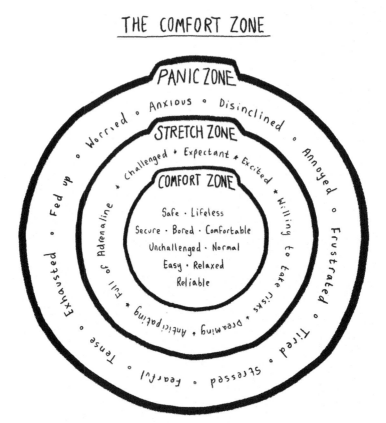

You may also recall when you knew you were ready to step outside of the comfort of your classroom; when you knew you were ready to take on increased responsibilities. The classroom walls had become too small for you and were constricting your growth.

It was because you acknowledged your feelings while within your comfort zone and chose to step into your so-called stretch zone that you are a school leader today. The stretch zone is the area in our lives where we recognise a potential for growth and deeper realisation of our skills and talents.

Moving out of the comfort zone and into the stretch zone

Stepping out of your comfort zone into the position you are in today may have felt like a conscious decision, but it takes a far deeper level of consciousness to know how to thrive and survive in the stretch zone. It also takes a deeper level of consciousness to prevent it becoming a panic zone! In the panic zone, life is very, very hard. We lose all sense of perspective; we feel as though we are forever living on a knife edge. Our capacity to lead ourselves or others is severely limited.

It is never easy moving out of a comfort zone, where our self-esteem receives regular boosts when our expertise is recognised and validated by others. In the stretch zone, we have no immediate expertise to call upon. In the stretch zone, it is our self-esteem that feels under threat. We are no longer able to gain confidence from tasks, roles and responsibilities that we have yet to master. We have to admit that we do not know, and self-doubt and diminished self-confidence accompany these admissions.

Unfortunately 'not knowing' is often mistaken 'for not being able'. This is partly because, in order to protect ourselves from the pain of personal change, we adopt what soon become limiting defence mechanisms. These are behaviours that limit both our own and other people's perceptions of us.

By contrast, when support (as described in Chapter 2) is given, the stretch zone becomes a place in which growth can occur. Jungian analyst James Hollis argues that when we develop the capacity to accept and work with the anxiety and ambiguity that often accompanies movement outside our comfort zone, we in effect grow up.

Move into unfamiliar territory and anxiety is activated as our constant comrade ... psychological or spiritual development always requires a greater capacity in us for the toleration

*of anxiety and ambiguity. The capacity to accept this state,
abide it and commit to life is the more measure of maturity.*
Hollis (2006)

In accepting this truth, we accept that life is not always easy.
And in the context of school leadership, we also accept that
struggle is as much about our own maturity and growth as
it is about the maturity and growth of our schools and those
we lead and manage.

Strangers to ourselves

In the stretch zone it is also possible for us to become
strangers to ourselves. We want to know how to befriend
ourselves again, but our emotions, our feelings and our
experiences are taking us to places within ourselves that we
have never been to before. As a result, we have none of our
familiar responses to bring us back to our old familiar selves.
We are changing, and personal change scares us.

   If the right support is not forthcoming when we are in
our stretch zone, we often experience a threat to our self-
esteem. If our self-esteem needs (such as the need to feel
worthy, valued and accepted (Chapter 1) are not met, we can
experience a debilitating sense of self-doubt. Our minds
may be plagued with questions as we seek to understand the
turbulent process of shaping a new identity. We ask ourselves:

- Who am I now?
- Have I got what it takes to succeed?
- Why don't I understand?
- What am I doing wrong?
- Will I always feel like this?
- Why does everything take so long and feel so difficult?

If our questions remain unanswered, the distance between
who we are and what we could be becomes greater. Feeling
unsure of how best to cope, we may retreat to the relative

safety of our comfort zone, thus halting the transformation process in its tracks. Or we may choose to face our fears, to find answers to our questions from those who are willing to listen and support us; in so doing, we learn day by day that it is possible to positively embrace the struggle of personal transformation.

Feelings in the stretch zone

In the stretch zone our feelings are varied. They can be divided into positive and negative.

Positive feelings	Negative feelings
Excitement	Anxiety
Optimism	Nervousness
Hope	Self-doubt
Joy	Worry
Enthusiasm	Fear
Confidence	Disinclination

Pause for a moment and reflect on the time that you first stepped into the role you are in now. How did you feel?

I vividly remember how I felt on my first day as a Headteacher – a mixture of excitement, optimism and hope, mixed with a good dose of anxiety, nervousness and fear. I was excited and full of hope about the plans I had for the children in my school and what could be done to take the school out of special measures. But I was fearful too. I was one of the youngest members of staff: how would the others respond to me? I knew that one of the reasons I had been appointed was my people skills, but I knew my conflict management skills were in need of development! I was great at handling conflict and breaking up fights and disagreements among children, but with adults – that was another matter!

Stepping into the role of Headteacher meant that for the time it would take me to learn this new skill (among others), I would be living and leading from my stretch zone.

Finding your feet

When leaders change roles and step out of their comfort zones, it can take a while for them to regain their equilibrium. It certainly took me some time to really feel the role of Headteacher belonged to me and that I could take it, shape it and make it my own.

For a new school leader, or an experienced school leader in a new role, the experience is much the same. New school environments to get used to; new relationships to be built; new structures and systems to develop; and all needing enormous investments of time and energy. When the pace of change is swift, many school leaders give the appearance of coping when in fact they are just managing to keep their heads above water (Figure 5.2). Behind the calm, external veneer, their emotions are in turmoil as they 'try to find ways' to keep their inner fears and doubts at bay.

Figure 5.2: Keeping head above the water

Hidden fears

As a new Headteacher, I harboured a secret fear that only those nearest and dearest to me knew about. When I was at school, I had always been told I would never be more than a nursery nurse; in fact, my careers teacher told me even that was too high an aspiration, and I should consider working on the tills in the supermarket. And here I was, fifteen years later – a Headteacher! However, the secret fear that had been planted during my teenage years had grown subconsciously. Maybe, just maybe, I wasn't good enough? Somewhere deep within my psyche was a vulnerable teenage schoolgirl who had been told she would never amount to anything. And now I had to learn how to shake off this limiting belief and accompanying self-doubt and fear so that I could step confidently into my role as Headteacher, and own it.

So here I was, moving into my stretch zone and not quite knowing how my mixed feelings and emotions would impact on my ability to lead. I was at the beginning of a learning curve and had no idea just how steep the incline was going to be!

How our biographies determine our performance in different zones

I know I am not alone in having to come to terms with how my past impacted upon my present. For more than a few of us, our biographies have been written with the words of those who thought less of us. Thanks to Stephen Covey, I have since come to realise that their words were:

... more projections than reflections, projecting the concerns and character weaknesses of people giving the input rather than accurately reflecting what we are.
Covey (1989)

As children, we have no way of knowing this. We have neither the language nor life experience to tell us not to take these words to heart. It is not until we are adults that we find ourselves in positions where we need to take a long, hard look at ourselves and, if we are lucky enough, discover the truth of who we really are.

If you are to survive in the stretch zone as a school leader, you need to be able to find your own truth and, every day, align your words, behaviours and actions to the fulfilment of that truth. You also need to be able to do this for the children in your school, so that they too can learn how to stretch the boundaries of their worlds, and become who they were born to be.

Your inner voice—friend or foe?

Many people stay in this inner space because they have not learnt how to turn down the volume, or to switch off their own critical inner voice. Through its constant pestering, nagging and criticism, that inner voice can cause you to believe that your false expectations will become reality. The fact is that they never really do, but your own inner monologue never really tells you that story – it has its own spin on reality. It tells you that your worst fears need your attention; it causes you to see the negative, as opposed to the positive, of any new situation; it reasons with you that things might be even worse the next time you find yourself in a stressful situation. Consequently, it tells you that it's best if you remain in a state of high alert, always vigilant, always on the lookout, always ready to face your greatest fear.

Of course this is madness! It is emotionally draining to remain in a state of high alert for something that might never happen. However, because you believe that your inner voice is looking out for your best interests, you succumb to its advice and inadvertently create for yourself a negative cycle of self-fulfilling prophecies.

Fear and your comfort zone

A key reason for a prolonged stay in the comfort zone is, quite simply, the fear of change. Fear can be disguised in many forms.

- It can be the churning feeling in the pit of your stomach when you think about things being different.
- It can be that sudden urgent need to take the dog for a walk or to watch *X Factor* or anything that will turn your mind away from moving out of your comfort zone.
- It can be the worst-case scenarios that you create in your head: *'What if things go wrong or don't turn out as I planned?'*
- It can be an inner voice that says: *'But really I am happy as things are. I don't want things to change'.*

When no one is challenging you to think differently, listening to your own inner voice, and its attempts to 'protect' you from hurt and pain, seems like a pretty sensible idea. However, when unexamined and left to run riot in your head, these voices can actually cause more harm than good. They act as invisible chains, binding you to ways of thinking and behaving that, over time, limit your growth and development. We call these voices our 'inner demons' in jest, but really, there is nothing funny about harbouring negative thoughts and feelings that prevent you from fulfilling your true potential.

From stretch zone to panic zone

The worst thing we can do in the stretch zone is to become defensive and deny to ourselves the reality of what we are feeling. We deem it to be too risky to reveal the truth to ourselves (or others). Alas, many of our defence mechanisms do not serve us well. What we most need from others (that is, support) we deny ourselves, by pushing others away. We become strangers to ourselves.

This can lead to a situation in which we find ourselves moving from the stretch zone into the panic zone, without having learnt all that we fully need to thrive in the stretch zone. Without proper supervision and support, our stretch zone can become our panic zone. We experience the panic zone when we feel overwhelmed by changes that originated in the stretch zone.

In the panic zone, we feel out of control and out of our depth. We experience feelings of anxiety, disinclination, annoyance, frustration, fear and exhaustion. In the panic zone, it is impossible for us to perform at our best.

Staying busy ... in the stretch zone

I have referred to the work of Brené Brown previously. In her book, *Daring Greatly: How the Courage to be Vulnerable Transforms the Way We Live, Love, Parent and Lead*, she makes the point that if we keep running from ourselves – if we allow ourselves to adopt behaviours that keep us from knowing who we are inside – we put limits on how we 'show up' in this world. She says of her own self:

I stayed so busy that the truth of my hurting and fear could never catch up. I looked brave on the outside and felt scared on the inside.
Brown (2012)

To live life fully in the stretch zone, we have to be able to show up in this world, to face our fears and have 'the courage to be vulnerable'. By learning to see our vulnerabilities as strengths, we can discover the lessons to be learnt and the meanings to be derived from our own different life experiences.

Discovering meaning and developing authenticity in the stretch zone

As the challenges of leadership increase, there can be an increased desire or need to try and create some sort of meaning out of what we are experiencing. In unfamiliar territory, the need for strategies that help us understand what we are going through becomes an important survival tool.

Things we were once so sure of about ourselves or our context now seem uncertain, and we scrabble around in the darkness for answers. As meaning and sense seem to fall from our grasp, we experience the impact this has on our own psychological well-being. There is a basic human need to be able to derive meaning from life's events.

Numerous authors have described deriving meaning from events as a 'fundamental human motive'. The benefits to finding meaning in events range from an increased will to live [...] to perceiving benefits in specific stressful events.
Arnold *et al.* (2007)

Coaching and regaining control in the stretch zone

Learning to feel safe in the sometimes destabilising area of the stretch zone is also about how we learn to gain a sense of being in control.

When we say to ourselves, 'I've never been here before' and experience the associated feelings of fear, anxiety and self-doubt, we have to find a way to turn events and emotions on their head. We have to find a way of saying, *'I have never been here before, but I believe I have what it takes to get through this'*. When we are able to do this, we experience the positive emotions that come from the psychological position of self-empowerment.

In an article published by *The Harvard Business Review (2010)*, 'Moments of greatness', the American business coach, Robert E. Quinn, describes his process for enabling top executives to step with confidence into the stretch zone.

1. Recognise that you have already been there.
2. Analyse your current state.
3. Ask yourself four key questions:
   - Am I results centred?
   - Am I internally directed?
   - Am I other-focused?
   - Am I externally open?

The steps Quinn identifies are based on the premise that all leaders will have experienced 'peak moments', or what he describes as 'the fundamental state', at some stage in their careers. This state may or may not have been born out of crisis, but nevertheless, when guided by our deepest values, it enables us to perform at our best. Details of his process are outlined below, with additional questions (5 and 6) based upon my own work with school leaders.

Robert E. Quinn's process for entering the fundamental state of leadership

a) Recognise you've already been there
You've faced challenges before and, in surmounting them, you entered the fundamental state. By recalling the lessons of this state, you can release positive emotions and see new possibilities for your current situation.

b) Analyse your current state
Compare your normal performance with what you did at your very best. You'll fuel a desire to elevate what you're doing now and generate confidence that you can re-enter the fundamental state.

c) Ask four key questions
The purpose and intention of each questions is outlined in the chart below.

BY ASKING ...	YOU SHIFT FROM ...	TO ...
1. Am I results centred? *In a school context, the answer will always be 'Yes', so I would amend this to:* While focusing on results what else do I also need to be centred on?	Remaining in your comfort zone and solving familiar problems	Moving to possibilities that don't yet exist
2. Am I internally directed?	Complying with others' expectations and conforming to existing conditions	Clarifying your core values, acting with authenticity and confidence, and willingly initiating productive approaches to problem-solving
3. Am I other-focused?	Allowing pursuit of your own self-interest to shape your relationships	Committing to the collective good in your organisation
4. Am I externally open?	Controlling your environment, making incremental changes and relying on established routines	Learning from your environment and acknowledging (when necessary) the need for major change and adjustments to routines

I have some more questions to add:

BY ASKING ...	YOU SHIFT FROM ...	TO ...
Who do I want to be?	The feelings of distress associated with the challenges of your present reality	Keeping focused on the best vision that you have of yourself
Who believes in me?	Self-doubt	Focusing on evidence provided by others that validates your skill and achievements
Where can I look for support?	Feeling that you have to struggle alone	Being proactive and seeking out others who will support you through your challenges

When facing difficult and stressful times, such an approach can help us to find:

- Meaning – Courage – Purpose – Inner strength
- Direction – Hope – Resilience – Self-belief

The incorporation of such tools into our day-to-day lives helps us develop a deeper sense of what it means to be an authentic leader and to live a life comfortable with ambiguity, and with the strength, knowledge and wisdom to embrace the challenge of school leadership.

STOP, PAUSE AND REFLECT

Summary points:

- Change is a necessary part of the personal and professional growth process.

- When we step out of our comfort zones, we need support that will enable us to thrive in the stretch zone.
- Wisdom and courage in the stretch zone are cultivated when we ask questions of ourselves that challenge the way in which we think and cause us to see other possibilities.

EXERCISE

Reflect on the diagram of the comfort zone (Figure 5.3).

Figure 5.3: My current performance zone

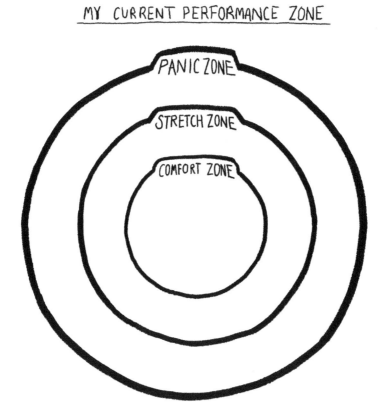

MY CURRENT PERFORMANCE ZONE

PANIC ZONE

STRETCH ZONE

COMFORT ZONE

In the comfort zone circle:

1. Write down all the events you have had to deal with as a leader that you now feel comfortable handling.
2. Write down any events you are currently facing that have required you to step outside your comfort zone.
3. For the events you have listed, ask yourself the following questions:
   - What have I done to improve my confidence/competence in handling these situations?
   - What has been the outcome?
   - What else can I do to help improve my confidence/competence in handling these situations?
   - What will be the benefits to me and my school when I take these actions?

CHAPTER 6:
Decluttering the Mind

You are today where the thoughts of yesterday have brought you and you will be tomorrow where the thoughts of today will take you.

**Blaise Pascal
(French mathematician, physicist, writer and philosopher)**

Decluttering the Mind

In this chapter you will discover:
- How the role of the coach differs from other professional relationships.
- How a coaching conversation can help you move from where you are now to where you want to be.
- The key theories and principles underpinning coaching conversations and how to apply them when seeking to resolve your own leadership challenges.

Having a coach offers benefits beyond simply honing leadership skills. It gives you another set of eyes and ears and so can be an antidote to the peril of the information quarantine that too many leaders suffer. Coaches help you to see outside the balloon of your daily experience.
Goleman (2003a)

Goleman's remark begs the question: What is it about the role of a coach that sets it apart from other professional relationships, in enabling leaders to see outside of the balloon of their daily experience?

To answer this question, I want to begin by:

- giving a brief overview of the roots of coaching.
- looking at the way in which the coaching role differs from other professional relationships school leaders are likely to have.
- looking at some of the key theories and principles that coaches apply in their work.

This information will enable you not only to understand the role of the coach, but also to appreciate how their approach differs from more traditional support processes.

The roots of coaching

Coaching has its roots in the work of two 1950s psychologists – Carl Rogers and Abraham Maslow – and their concept of humanistic psychology.

People have choices and want to exercise them. Coaches invite clients to be architects of their own future selves by taking choices and responsibility for those choices.
O'Conner and Lages (2007)

This is precisely why, when people talk about coaching, they speak about a process that leads them to feeling empowered. When we are empowered:

- We feel in control of our life and circumstances.
- We know how to access our own internal resources to bring about personal change.
- We understand the actions that we ourselves must take in order to move us towards our desired future.
- We feel understood, and in being understood we come to a greater understanding of ourselves and who we are as individuals.

This way of being with another person involves accepting that their experience of the world is unique and is to be valued and respected. No comparisons with other people or judgements are made. The relationship is solely about how they experience life and what it means for them to be human. It is a journey of self-discovery or, as Maslow would describe, a journey towards 'self-actualisation'.

Man's desire for fulfilment, namely the tendency for him to become actually what he is potentially; to become everything that one is capable of becoming.
Maslow (quoted in O'Conner and Lages, 2007)

How the coach role differs from other professional support roles

From a mentor

Having a mentor is particularly useful when you are new in role and need to learn from someone who has been there before. We understand that a mentor is normally someone who has a wealth of professional experience; who is willing to share their experience and their skills and knowledge with you in order that you might learn from them. The expertise that a coach brings to the relationship is different. It is their ability to listen deeply and to ask high-level questions that enable you to become an expert in understanding and leading yourself that sets the coach apart from the mentor. A coach believes that you can sit at the feet of your own learning experience and, through structured reflection and dialogue, create your own personalised continuing professional development (CPD) pathway that centres on the lessons learnt from your own leadership practice.

From a school advisor

Generally speaking, school advisors are there to give you advice on how to run your school. Very often their role includes monitoring and evaluation of data. Because they are held accountable for your success, they often have an ambiguous position and may make a narrowly subjective assessment of you and your school. In contrast, a coach has no agenda to meet other than your own. Coaches are totally impartial, with no other person to report back to, other than themselves or a supervisor. Their supervisor will ensure that the integrity of their coaching relationships is preserved and also that professional boundaries are maintained. In this respect, a coach works confidentially with you, listening to and respecting your judgements, while helping you to see things from new angles and devise solutions that you feel are the best fit for you and your school.

From a school governor

Governors play a crucial role in the life of a school and, when the relationship works well, their place as 'critical friend' can be an immense support for a school leader, particularly for those in the Headteacher role. Yet the term 'critical friend' suggests a relationship that involves a degree of vulnerability and openness. Let's be honest, because you are accountable to your governing body, this is hard to achieve, and Headteachers who have this type of relationship with their governors are often in the minority. A coach, however, can become a trusted confidante, a person who will allow you to step safely outside of the 'information quarantine' and discuss in great depth the twin aspects of your own leadership journey and your school's performance.

How coaching works: Understanding key theories and principles

State-related learning

Coaches use various models that enable leaders and managers to develop the mental acuity required to deal with the demands their roles. One of the reasons that coaching is such a powerful form of support is that it recognises how the state of mind you learn in differs from the state of mind you need when you are in a leadership role. Amid the everyday stresses and pressures of your normal work environment, you are often in a state of 'high alert': a state in which acquiring new knowledge is removed from your day-to-day experience. This partly explains why, on returning to work after a training course, only a small fraction of what was learnt is usually retained and acted upon.

Coaching differs because it involves one-to-one reflections on learning, on practice and on theory, and on the integration of all constituent parts. Thus, it helps leaders develop the neural pathways that will allow them to remain cool under pressure and maximise their ability to perform at their best – even in the most trying of circumstances.

Putting the theory into practice

The best way to illustrate the points I have made so far is through a case study showing how theory and practice impact upon each other during the coaching process. In education we are used to discussing Kolb's learning cycle (Figure 6.1) as a way to help us understand the adult learning process. When applied to coaching, we can see just how powerful a tool this is for supporting leadership learning on the job.

Kolb's cycle clarifies what happens when adults are engaged in learning and change, and outlines an explicit process for reflection and guidance through stages that enables each person to:

- gain deeper understanding of new experiences within a specific situation or context
- extrapolate new meaning from their personal reflections on the experience
- devise and experiment with new behaviours and ways of being to enhance future personal development and growth.

Figure 6.1: Kolb's learning cycle

This case study is that of Shona, an experienced inner-city Headteacher who has been in the profession for over fourteen years.

CASE STUDY—Shona's learning journey

Shona was asked to take on the role of executive Headteacher at a local school, St John's. It was not performing well and was without a Headteacher. A soft federation with Shona's school meant that in addition to being head of her own school, she would invest time in working collaboratively with the governors and teachers of St John's to develop successful strategies for moving the school forward. Anyone in a similar situation knows that creating a structure to facilitate this type of working arrangement requires a great deal of change, and new working relationships and systems need to be tested, reviewed and implemented. However, the support Shona required was not related to any operational and structural changes needed to make this initiative a success; she needed support to help her make sense of the unexpected personal transitions that occurred in her relationships with herself and with others.

Change starts with me

Shona was very astute in recognising that the flip-side of the change process was to do with developing a better understanding of her own personal responses to change. Before coaching began, she had already identified the practicalities of her new role; they weren't an issue. She knew systems, she knew processes, and she could do school improvement plans in her sleep! What she couldn't do was make sense of the tangled web of thoughts and emotions that accompanied her new role.

So at the start of the coaching process it was agreed that there would be two key objectives for her coaching sessions:
- To develop new ways of being in order to balance the personal and professional demands of her new role.
- To understand new self-perceptions that occurred as her professional identities changed.

Approach
The coaching sessions made use of Kolb's learning cycle in the following ways.

Stage 1—Concrete experience
Stage 1 of Kolb's cycle is where someone is engaged in something that requires them to adopt specific behaviours; it is normally the place where the reflective learning cycle begins. In Shona's case, the experience that formed the basis for reflection within the coaching sessions was being the head of a soft federation and managing the inter- and intra-personal transitions that occurred as a result. Shona had not anticipated that the way in which she saw herself would change; neither had she anticipated the degree to which her relationships with members of her senior leadership team would alter.

Stage 2—Reflective observation
When someone is engaged in new learning, the experience will have an impact at both emotional and rational levels, leaving a range of feelings and thoughts about the experience. If left as a collection of emotions and 'head talk', it is unlikely that learning of any real depth will occur. People need to be given opportunities to reflect on what they have experienced to ensure that new (and perhaps more desirable) outcomes can be achieved in the future. In the busy lives of school leaders, this does not always happen; they simply do not have the time and space to reflect on day-to-day events, and find themselves in a cycle where old behaviours continue to produce the same (sometimes disappointing) results. Reflective observation within Kolb's cycle allows a person:
- to step outside the situation and reflect, as an observer, on what they experienced
- to come to terms with their feelings about their circumstances.

At this stage in the learning cycle, a number of key questions come into play as the coach works with them to help them gain a greater understanding and as complete a picture as possible of what they have experienced. In coaching Shona, it was integral to the process to ask questions that enabled her to think honestly through her very current reality of managing two schools and what this meant for her on a personal level. The type of questions that were asked at this stage were:

- What expectations did you have of your new role?
- How have your expectations changed?
- What has this experience meant for you?
- How have others responded to your change in role and how have you responded to them?
- What have been the key areas of learning for you?
- What have you learnt about yourself personally?
- What impact has this change in role had upon you?

Through guided reflection, supported through questions like these, Shona became more discerning about her situation; she saw events more clearly and plotted a clearer path forward. She was able to see that not only had the change in role caused her to view the role of Headteacher differently, but it had also caused her to start thinking and behaving differently. She saw these changes as positive, because she was starting to develop sides of herself that had hitherto lain dormant; she was becoming more assertive, listening and responding to her own needs. However, others found these changes in behaviour disconcerting – they were used to the 'old' Shona. Changes in her behaviour meant they had to change too.

Stage 3—Abstract conceptualisation

This is the stage in Kolb's cycle where the learner is invited to draw conclusions from their reflections and identify what the experience has taught them. When the experience has involved other people, they are encouraged to 'theorise' on what they have learnt about themselves, what they have learnt about others, and how this new knowledge can be used to inform future decisions. Within coaching this is often an 'Aha!' or light-bulb moment for the client, as they realise that they had the answers all along to their current problems. They also realise that if they were to face the same scenario again, they could encounter it with new knowledge and insight, which if acted upon could result in different or more favourable outcomes.

For Shona, the realisation was that if she felt mixed up and confused as she tried to process everything that was happening to her, then it was likely that those closest to her – other senior leaders across both schools – were likely to be feeling the same way. She also came to understand that sometimes their negative behaviours and responses were not necessarily personal attacks; more often than not, they were an unconscious expression of the fear they felt, and as yet they had no conscious means or structured approach (as she acquired through the coaching) for expressing it.

Stage 4—Active experimentation
Kolb's model is cyclical. Once the individual moves to active experimentation and starts to test out new behaviours, he or she moves once again into Stage 1, the experiencing phase. This leads to a continual process of reflection on the outcomes of new behaviours, adapting and making changes where necessary. As this person experiences a number of iterations of the cycle, he or she becomes more open to change and the opportunities for self-reflection and development that can be derived from being placed in new situations.

Armed with personal knowledge and insight gained in her coaching sessions, Shona facilitated open discussions with her senior leaders, which created a safe space for them to talk honestly about what they were feeling and what the changes meant for them on a personal level. As a result, Shona succeeded in creating highly self-aware teams across both of her schools. These teams weren't afraid to express their vulnerabilities and knew which behaviours and attitudes they would need to adopt to secure successful outcomes for all.

What were the outcomes for Shona?

We do not receive wisdom; we must discover it for ourselves.
Marcel Proust (quoted in Lee, 2003)

Coaching enabled Shona to develop new ways of thinking, of being and doing. It was the start of a journey that led to new and heightened levels of self-discovery and awareness. As Shona reflected at the end of the process: *'Coaching far exceeded my expectations. Somehow you managed to draw out of me answers to the questions that I had in my head. I was able to rationalise what was going on across the two schools ... what you did was, you gave me time and space to find myself, and I have come out a better person.'*

Applying the process to you

Kolb's learning cycle provided Shona with the map for the process, but it was a key coaching model that provided the tools that enabled her to reach the other side. The key coaching model used was the TGROW model, as illustrated in Figure 6.2, where TGROW stands for Topic – Goal – Reality – Options – Will/Wrap up.

Figure 6.2: The TGROW model

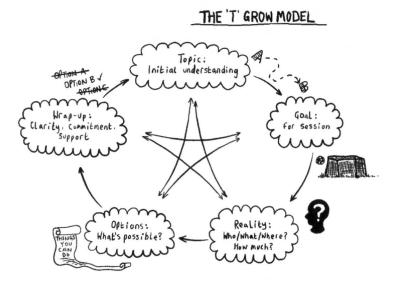

The TGROW model is a fantastic coaching tool that provides a very clear pathway for helping someone get from where they are at a certain point to where they want to be. A coach who is skilled in its use can be an invaluable resource for a school leader who doesn't need:

- to be given advice
- to be told what to do
- to be instructed
- to be judged;

but who needs or wants:

- to find their own solutions
- clarify their own thoughts
- to own and take charge of their own decisions.

My intention with the last few pages of this chapter is to give you an overview of the model, as well as some questions to accompany each stage. In those rare quiet moments when it's just you and your own thoughts and you have a problem that needs resolving, you can turn to these pages and work through the process to uncover your own solution for whatever challenge you may be facing.

STAGE 1—TOPIC:
Initial understanding of what you want to explore

The coach begins by asking you to introduce the 'topic' and to set the context for whatever it is you wish to bring to the session. By doing so, he or she offers you an invitation to 'open up', to talk freely about whatever issues you would like to think through. At this stage of the conversation, the coach is seeking to understand your context and your issue, so they are able to walk alongside you on your leadership journey.

Consider the following 'topic' questions:

- What is the issue that you are currently dealing with?

- How long has this been an issue or concern for you?
- What impact is it having?

STAGE 2—Goal:
What do you want to get out of the session? What is your desired outcome?

In the Goal stage of the conversation, the coach helps you think about how you would like things to be – your desired outcome. When you set goals, you begin the process of setting yourself up for success. Goals give:

- A clear sense of direction: You know where you are heading and are therefore far less likely to be knocked off course; and even when you are, you know the path that will take you back to where you want to get to.
- A focus for where and how you invest your time and energy: No longer are your thoughts and actions dispersed and erratic. Clear goals give clarity of thought. With greater clarity comes greater wisdom as to how your time can be used in pursuit of your goals.
- A sense of purpose: When your goals are fully aligned with your role, your sense of purpose and your drive to achieve are far greater. 'Why' is foremost in your mind and as a result you experience greater alignment between your thoughts, words and actions.
- Security: When you work towards clearly defined and meaningful goals, you get a sense that, even with ups and downs, all will eventually be well. This added sense of security is part of what helps you get up and keep moving forward, despite the frequent falls and knockbacks.

Consider the following GOAL questions:

- What is the goal that you want to achieve?
- What will it mean when you have achieved your goal?
- When do you want to have achieved your goal?
- How will you know that your goal has been achieved?

- What will be different?
- What will you see?
- What will you hear?
- What will you feel?

STAGE 3—Reality:
Gaining a clear picture of where things are now

Once you have defined where you want to get to, you will look at the reality of your current situation. This helps you form a very clear picture of whatever it is you have brought to the coaching conversation. When faced with a dilemma, a million thoughts can go round and round in your head, until it feels like a plate full of spaghetti (Figure 6.3). It can be hard to untangle one thought from another. There appears to be no beginning and no end. Everything is a jumbled mess. We simply cannot think straight!

Figure 6.3: Spaghetti dilemma

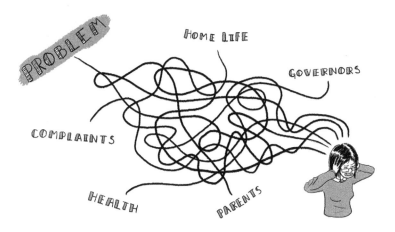

The coach will help you untangle your thoughts, to unravel the constituent parts of your situation, and help you see:

- The role that you have played.
- The role that others have played.
- The relationship between different parties.
- The impact of conversations and actions.
- How the pieces of the jigsaw puzzle fit together.

Consider the following REALITY questions:

- What actions have you taken to try and resolve your current challenge?
- What has been the outcome?
- What have you learnt?
- What role have others played in this issue?
- What role have you played?
- What has been the outcome?

Once you have a clear sense of where you want to get to (Goal) and how the current context (Reality) relates, either positively or negatively, to the achievement of your goal, then you are in much better position, psychologically, to begin thinking about how your goal will be achieved.

STAGE 4—Options:
Deciding on the choices you will make

Without an objective outside voice, we very often find ourselves putting a self-imposed limit on what is possible. Rarely do we question that inner voice that says: *'Don't try that – you'll look foolish'* or *'You know it won't work. Best play safe and do what you've always done.'* As a result, many of us only achieve a fraction of what we could achieve in our lives. As James Hollis says:

The struggle for growth is not for us alone; it is not self-indulgent. It is our duty and service to those around us as

*well, for through such departures from the comfortable we
bring a larger gift to them.*
Hollis (2006)

Consider the following OPTIONS questions:

- What actions could you take to help you achieve
  your goal?
- Which actions appeal to you the most?
- Which actions would have the greatest impact on you
  achieving your goal?
- What else could you do?
- If you knew you wouldn't be judged or criticised what
  actions might you take?

For the last question, list or write on sticky notes any options
that come into your head – try really hard not to self-censor
or to listen to that voice that says: *'Don't be silly!'* You may
surprise yourself by the new ideas that spring to mind. What
would a mind map of your different options look like? Have
a go at drawing one.

STAGE 5—Will/Wrap-up:
Committing to action to move you forward
Once you have explored all your options, the coach will move
with you to the final stage of the conversation, where you
are supported to see which of your options has the greatest
chance of success. Nothing is imposed on you. The coach
remains fixed on helping you decide your own actions, and
helps you plot an action plan for success – a plan that you
own and feel happy and confident to carry out.
  Consider the following WILL/WRAP UP questions:

- Which of your options do you think will help you achieve
  your goal?
- In what priority order would you place your options?

- What actions would need to be placed alongside your options in order for them to become a reality?
- What date would you put next to your actions steps?
- Is there anyone else that needs to be involved in helping you to take action?
- What are the success criteria for your action steps?
- What will be the benefit for you when your actions are complete?
- What will be the benefit for others?
- How will you reward yourself when the goal is achieved?
- And (just so you are prepared for the inevitable curve balls!): Can you foresee any obstacles that might get in the way of you taking your actions?
- How might you address them?

I have seen the magic in this model happen time and time again. School leaders – whose heads were so full of their own and other people's 'stuff' that they couldn't think straight – who when given a quiet, confidential space to process their thoughts in, then experienced greater levels of:

- Clarity
- Energy
- Confidence
- Self-belief.

As one of my clients succinctly put it:
'Coaching has been like oxygen for my brain!'

Figure 6.4: Oxygen for the brain

STOP, PAUSE AND REFLECT

Summary points:

- Coaching has its roots in humanistic psychology, which works with and seeks to find the good in people.
- Coaching is a relationship built on mutual trust and respect, where the coachee owns both the agenda and the outcomes for the sessions.
- Coaching empowers each person to find their own solutions by asking questions that help clarify their thought processes and de-clutter their mind.

CHAPTER 7:
Bringing Out the Best in Others

When we seek to discover the best in others, we somehow bring out the best in ourselves.

**William Arthur Ward
(American writer, poet and inspirationist)**

Bringing Out the Best in Others

In this chapter you will discover:
- Why our life scripts sometimes hamper our ability to communicate effectively.
- Why most performance management systems fail and what can be done about it.
- The key interpersonal skills that all senior leaders need to develop if they are to excel in developing their capacity to bring out the best in others.

The frustrations, pressures, and challenges teachers face test their self-esteem, energy and dedication every day. To preserve throughout their careers the vision with which the best of them started – to hold fast to the idea that the business they are in is that of setting minds on fire – is a heroic project.
Branden (1994)

It is a project that all teachers and school leaders face; it is about learning to bring out the best in themselves and others. It is as much about ensuring their pupils are emotionally intelligent, as it is about ensuring they are numerate and literate. It is about ensuring their pupils leave school with levels of emotional maturity and insight that will enable them to develop positive relationships with people from all walks of life. It is about a human quest, in which the prize should not just be a ranking on government league tables, but the building of generations of young people who possess a healthy sense of self-worth and belief in their own capabilities and potential, ready to stride forward and to make their own dreams a reality.

All schools hold the potential for helping young people realise that a different type of humanity exists from that which they might experience outside of school. This is particularly true for inner-city schools, where the fragility of human relationships may be manifested through the challenging behaviours of the children and their parents.

For a school to realise its potential of being a place in which humanity is at its best (and by extension, a place where all human beings flourish), a school has to be an emotionally healthy place in which all the adults within the community possess a positive sense of self and have robust emotional maturity. Yet, sadly, we know this is very hard to achieve. Why? Because very few adults, leaders included, are the 'complete package'. Many have issues that relate to their own self-esteem and the degree to which they value themselves.

On a daily basis, many teachers and school leaders are adept at delivering creative and dynamic PHSE lessons, yet they – or to be more accurate, the system – is inept at helping them apply these lessons to themselves; lessons that are necessary if they are to maintain a healthy and robust self-esteem and rise above the often bruising pressures of school life. Nathaniel Branden author of *The Six Pillars of Self Esteem*, argues (and I would agree) that:

If their goal is to nurture self-esteem in those entrusted in their care, teachers ... like all of us, need to begin by working on their own.
Branden (1994)

Why is it that so many schools struggle to do this effectively, and people-management issues dominate the time of most school leaders? If it is not already evident from what you have read so far, quite simply my answer is that we humans are complex and the older we get, the harder it seems to be for us to truly grow up and behave as adults. Children are far easier to understand and deal with; even the most challenging are honest. Whether through their behaviour, or otherwise, they let us know how they are truly feeling.

The games people play

With us 'grown-ups', the communication games we played as children continue into adulthood and into our personal and professional lives. Most of the time, we are unaware of the roles that we and others adopt in the game. However, if you are a line manager, there will come a time when you shout:

'Stop! The rules of this game need to change!'

That's when you come to the realisation that, if you understood a little bit more about yourself and the dynamics of human behaviour, you'd have a far greater chance of being able to achieve better outcomes for yourself, and those you lead and manage.

Transactional analysis (TA)

Developed by Dr Eric Berne in the 1950s, TA is a psychological tool that can help us develop a greater understanding of what happens when we communicate with other people. An understanding of TA in our working lives can help us to:

- identify our emotional triggers and the emotional triggers of others
- overcome our emotional triggers and lead from a place of deep personal self-control, and
- better understand those we lead and manage and the strategies that we may need to adopt in order to get the best out of them.

In devising TA, Berne identified three 'ego states' (Figure 7.1) that dictate the way that we think, feel and behave when we communicate with others.

Figure 7.1: Three ego states

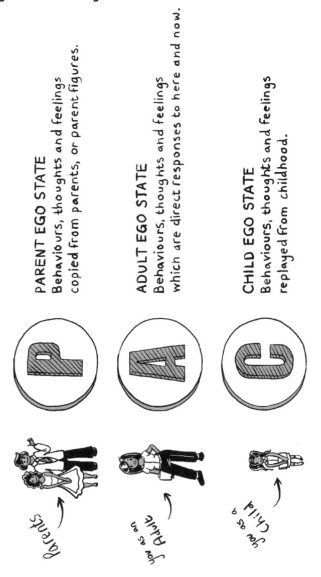

PARENT EGO STATE
Behaviours, thoughts and feelings copied from parents, or parent figures.

ADULT EGO STATE
Behaviours, thoughts and feelings which are direct responses to here and now.

CHILD EGO STATE
Behaviours, thoughts and feelings replayed from childhood.

Parents

You as an Adult

You as a Child

1. Parent ego state

These are the ways of thinking, feeling and responding to life's events that we learned from our parents and other authority figures (e.g. teachers and grandparents) in our formative years. They encompass the full spectrum of parenting experiences.

2. Adult ego state

The adult ego state is a place of power equality. There is no defending or attacking, because there is no sense of unbalanced power or inequality between individuals. When we are able to operate from the adult ego state we remain mindful. Our responses are in the present moment, in alignment with our vision of our best selves, and not unduly influenced by the past. We are able to remain objective in our interactions; there are no emotional hotspots or triggers to cloud communications. Everything is seen and heard as it is.

3. Child ego state

When we think, act and behave as the younger version of ourselves, and in certain situations replay behaviours (both positive and negative) from our childhood, we are adopting a child ego state.

Leaving aside the adult ego state, both the parent and child ego states have their pros and cons as illustrated in Figure 7.2.

Figure 7.2: The pros and cons of ego states

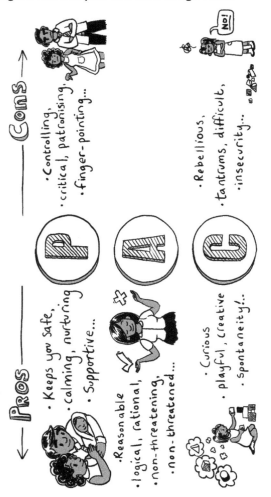

Becoming aware of our ego states

Most of the time, the ego states we adopt when we are working with others are subconscious. The theory is dependent upon our own personal histories; we each have a unique life script that influences the degree to which we adopt these different ego states. As a result, communication has the potential to become clouded if the people communicating with one another are unaware of them. Each person is responding to a subconscious emotional trigger that emanates from the child or parent ego state; sustained communication in either mode is not healthy for the individual or the relationship.

As a school leader, you have a responsibility for bringing out the best in yourself and others, therefore consciousness is essential. Even if others are not aware of the ego state they are operating from, you have a responsibility always to strive to engage with them from the adult ego state. Greater awareness and greater self-control will ultimately lead to better outcomes both for yourself and your staff, as illustrated in the case study below.

CASE STUDY—What happens when a nurturing parent ego state meets an attention-seeking child ego state

Jane was an assistant Headteacher and part of her role involved supporting a newly qualified teacher, Eva. Eva was very strong, with bags of potential, and it was evident that she was going to develop into a very capable teacher. However, she appeared to be in constant need of reassurance. She would find numerous ways to get Jane's attention, often eating into time that Jane had set aside for completing her own tasks. It reached a point where Jane knew something had to change. Her workload was increasing simply because she was giving more and more of her time to Eva.

As I listened to Jane – and in particular listened to how she was responding to Eva – it soon became evident that an attention-seeking child and nurturing-parent dynamic was at play. Jane's natural default position was always to provide solutions and overplay the nurturing parent role by putting other people's needs before her own.

As I encouraged Jane to reflect on her own behaviours in relation to Eva, she came to realise that her subconscious nursing and over-caring parenting stance was actually harming both herself and Eva. She was always available and always providing answers.

Jane came to see for herself that she was limiting the degree to which Eva could:
- develop her independence and self-belief
- make mistakes and learn from them
- develop her own levels of resilience and ability to problem solve.

And in relation to herself, she was limiting:
- the amount of time she could spend on attending to her own personal and professional needs
- her own capacity to develop a new leadership style and related behaviours
- her ability to manage her time and achieve a greater work–life balance.

Coaching enabled Jane to see that she had to step out of the 'nurturing parent' role and seek to move to the adult ego state when in dialogue with Eva. By doing so, she could help Eva learn to stand on her own feet and move away from the position of the attention-seeking child to adult. Without coaching to raise her levels of awareness, it would have been nearly impossible for Jane to recognise how her behaviours were compounding the situation. She would have continued to act out of a state of ignorance, perpetuating the child–parent transaction and being none the wiser about what she could have done to change the situation.

Performance management and bringing out the best in others

Performance management is an essential process that exists in schools for managing adult behaviour. However, the process is often seen as perfunctory, and in some cases is not seen as a significant driver to assist school improvement, therefore a real opportunity is missed for developing potential and bringing out the best in others. When line managers are skilled in using the principles of coaching to assist their performance management meetings, they help to create a clear path for developing a school culture in which there is an:

Organic sense of self-improvement fuelled by the genuine and self-motivated desire of all individuals to make things better.
Buck (2009)

When a school's culture matches this description, what is created is a set of common understandings and beliefs about performance management – with the potential to achieve school targets through:

- Creating alignment between organisational and personal objectives.
- Growing and developing other people.
- Enabling others to step outside their comfort zones.
- Supporting others to achieve their full potential.
- Inspiring confidence in other people's ability to succeed.
- Ensuring ownership and accountability.

When opposite beliefs and attitudes exist about the purpose and value of performance management, school cultures are created in which individuals:

- Struggle to take responsibility for their own actions.
- Become dependent on others for solutions and place limitations on their own ability to problem solve.
- Lack the internal motivation and desire to succeed.
- Weaken their ability to take risks and learn from their mistakes.

The simple truth is, when systems for performance management exist that do not develop a person's sense of self-worth, a void can be created between their perception of self and what they feel capable of achieving. In such environments, they either consciously or subconsciously limit what they give both to themselves and their school. Thus growth is restricted for themselves, those they lead and manage, and ultimately the pupils they teach.

This should never be allowed to happen. But sadly, we know it does.

Supporting confidence and personal growth

When coaching is placed firmly at the heart of the performance management process, teachers and other staff members experience a process in which belief in the development of human potential becomes central to the conversation.

People come to see more fully their unique role and the contributions they can make towards bringing about improvements in their school. Rather than seeing performance management as something that is done to them, they begin to understand what it means to be accountable to themselves and others, and they start to own the process. With self-accountability comes confidence and growth. With growth comes an increased sense of their own potential. When they have both confidence and a true sense of what might be, then a space is created for them to try to test out new behaviours.

Skills of the line manager

Coaching's surprisingly positive emotional impact stems largely from the empathy and rapport a leader establishes with employees. A good coach communicates a belief in a person's potential and an expectation that they can do their best. The tacit message is:

I believe in you. I'm investing in you, and I expect your best efforts. As a result, people sense that a leader cares, so they feel motivated to uphold their own standards for performance, and they feel accountable for how well they do.
Goleman (2003b)

For performance management to be meaningful and have a strong, direct impact on levels of staff motivation and improve standards for all, it is essential that those who carry out the task are both confident and competent in their ability to:

- Ask high-level questions.
- Listen for meaning.
- Be comfortable with a wide range of emotions.
- Enable staff to take ownership of objectives.
- Challenge staff to move out of their comfort zones.
- Manage their own emotions.
- Build others' confidence and self-belief.
- Identify others' self-limiting beliefs.

The importance of each of these factors in seeking to elicit the best from other people is discussed in the remaining pages of this chapter.

Asking high-level questions

Questions have the power to change both the content and direction of a conversation. Used as part of performance management procedures, questions play a key role in shaping the structure of the meeting and the quality of both the discussion and the targets or goals that are set. In performance management meetings, asking 'high-level' questions (ones that enable the person to think deeply about their intention and motivation to succeed) can be used to help both the member of staff and line manager to assess:

- Commitment to the bigger picture, school targets and goals.
- Levels of confidence and belief in an individual's ability to achieve.
- Resilience and ability to persist in the pursuit of targets and goals even in difficult situations.

The questions listed below are the type of questions that line managers might use to help ensure that the person remains on track, when working through targets that have been set for them as a result of the performance management process.

Questions to support performance management (based upon the GROW coaching model)

Goal
These questions enable teachers to identify the benefits for both the school and themselves when the objective is achieved:

- Why did you want to achieve this goal?
- What are the benefits for you now you have achieved this goal?
- How have you have achieved this goal?
- What are you hearing that tells you that you have achieved your goal?
- How are you feeling at this point in the future?
- What are you saying to yourself?
- When did you get there?
- What time-scale did it take?
- How did you know that you had achieved your goal?
- What measurement did you use?

Reality
Answers to these questions inform you about how confident the person feels in their ability to achieve objectives that have been set.

- What have you done so far to improve things?
- What were the results that you got from doing these things?
- What resources (e.g. skills, experience, qualifications, personal qualities) do you already have to help you to achieve your outcome?

Options

These questions prompt ideas about possible actions steps that can be taken to achieve an objective.

- What could you do to move yourself just one step forward right now?
- What appeals to you most about achieving this objective?
- What steps can you take that will give you that sense of satisfaction?
- What else could you do?

Will/Way Forward

These questions help commit to action.

- What are you going to do?

List the actions you must go through to meet this objective.

- How will these actions meet your main goal?
- When are you going to take these actions?
- What's the time-scale?
- How long do you think the list of actions will take you?
- Can you identify anticipated timescales for each item?
- Should anyone else be involved in this list of actions?
- When will you tell them?

Listening for meaning

Many conversations take place in school when only half of what the speaker says is fully heard or understood. Why is this? It is because we've become so used to giving the impression of listening that we have forgotten what it means to truly listen and to really hear what has been said. Our minds are so distracted by many things fighting for our attention – even in one-to-one situations. We do not realise that this can be a time to close the door, to re-direct our phone calls and pay full attention to the person in front of us and what they are saying. Schools are very busy places where the true act of listening is under-used; thus – although often unintended – staff members can feel neglected and unsupported.

Only when we truly master the art of listening can we hear and learn to understand what is being conveyed in the words, gestures, body language and 'silences' of others. When we can understand non-verbal communication and perceive the emotion behind a word or sentence, or see the message conveyed in a look to the side or a folded arm, we can enter into conversations that have far greater potential for development and growth. When we listen deeply, we create a space for the human spirit to be nurtured and we develop a greater understanding of what it means to be human.

Being comfortable with a wide range of emotions

Probably one of the biggest challenges faced by line managers is the range of emotions that can arise when dealing with underperforming staff. These members of staff are often angry, defensive, withdrawn and uncooperative. We probably all have a degree of expertise in dealing with these behaviours in our pupils, but when it comes to managing these behaviours in other adults, it is seriously hard work.

Line managers tend to adopt a range of coping strategies, such as avoidance, only giving positive and upbeat messages, or finding someone more senior to hold the other person to account. None of these approaches is satisfactory; they do not move the development of the manager or the staff member forward. Both are weakened through an inability to face challenging emotions head on.

In pursuit of excellence for our children, underperformance must be tackled. Being comfortable with the range of uncomfortable emotions that challenging scenarios evoke is key to schools excelling in the development of robust performance management procedures. Schools have to become better at being comfortable with uncomfortable feelings. As Brené Brown says, we have to become better at 'normalising discomfort'. For as long as we are unable to do this, we will ride roughshod, not only over our own feelings but also the feelings of others. The key is learning to do so in a humane way, and in a manner that protects the dignity of all involved.

Enabling staff to take ownership of objectives

If someone feels they have played a key role in setting performance management objectives, the chances of goals being fulfilled at the end of an academic year are far greater. An essential ingredient for success is ensuring that your performance management system (PMS) enables staff to connect with their 'moral purpose' – their reasons for being a part of your school and for being involved in the school's journey towards 'outstanding'.

You must ensure that your staff are involved in thinking about both their vision and their values, and are prepared to share this information with their line manager as part of the performance management procedure. The line manager must have a high degree of emotional intelligence and be able to create a 'safe place' for each of them to be heard. For some people, talking about vision, values and purpose can mean exposing their 'vulnerable' self. Yet this is the part of the self which, if addressed respectfully by the line manager, can result in someone being sufficiently motivated to set some of their own goals and achieve maximum levels of success for both themselves and the school.

Challenging staff to move out of their comfort zones

Within performance management, line managers need to be confident in their ability to use questions that help others move out of their comfort zones and try something new. They must have the skill set necessary to help staff face their fears, so that once their fears are placed out in the open, they can be supported in identifying strategies for overcoming them and making progress for both themselves and the school.

Managing your own emotions

This really is about your own level of emotional intelligence. How well tuned in you are to yourself. Do you give yourself enough time to stop and listen to your own emotions and the impact they may be having on yourself and others?

Emotions are contagious and in performance management meetings between two people, they are even more so. This is because your thoughts always impact on your feelings and your feelings always impact on your behaviours. So if you are feeling negative about the person, it is more likely that the outcome of your meeting will be negative. He or she will pick up on your negative energy and reflect it back at you, so that you both receive signals from each other that you are in an unsafe environment. The ensuing dialogue is one that takes place behind emotional and psychological defences, whereby each party seeks to protect their own sense of being and self-worth.

It is essential not to underestimate the impact that your own emotions can have on the outcomes of these meetings. If you are the line manager, it is imperative that prior to any performance management meeting you become attuned to your own emotions and what you feel about the person you will be meeting; if necessary, you should take action that will ensure you enter the meeting in a positive state of mind.

Building other people's confidence and self-esteem

Performance management can, if the right interpersonal skills are deployed, help build a person's sense of self and their confidence in their ability to succeed. As part of the process, performance management systems that facilitate growth in this area have stages that support individuals in identifying both their strengths and their areas for development. Opportunities for observation and feedback also form part of this process.

Feedback is a very important part of this process, because:

Without feedback there can be no transformative change. When we don't talk to the people we are leading about their strengths and opportunities for growth, they begin to question their contribution and our commitment [and] disengagement follows.
Brown (2012)

Through the feedback process we can help people both to celebrate their strengths and to tackle limiting beliefs and behaviours that may be holding them back. When we hear a teacher or another colleague say in response to feedback *'I can't'* or *'I know I can never be any good at such and such because...'* then we can intervene and help them reframe their thought processes, so that they think in terms of *'I can'* or *'This mistake has taught me x, y and z, so next time around I will try to ...'.*

When, as a line manager, you are able to help someone overcome a self-limiting belief, as with children, you enable them to see that:

- They are not prisoners of their past.
- They can create new possibilities of what can be for both themselves and others.
- It is possible to adopt new ways of thinking and behaving and succeed in the process.

By seeking to embed processes that develop human potential and feelings of self-worth, school leaders can begin to create cultures where leadership truly is devolved and everyone knows, owns and fully plays their part in bringing the vision alive.

STOP, PAUSE AND REFLECT

Summary points:

- We reduce the time spent on human process issues when time is invested in developing processes that cultivate people taking ownership of their actions.
- We bring out the best in others when we understand who they are and how our responses contribute to the dynamics of the relationship.
- A person-centred approach to performance management makes leaders of us all.

EXERCISE

This self-assessment is designed to help you, and other staff members who carry out performance management meetings, to assess where they are in the development of key skills and to identify what they need to do to address any areas for development.

Self-assessment of performance management skills

For each of the questions in italics below, score yourself on a scale of 1 to 10, where 1 is low and 10 is high.

High-level questions

- *How confident are you in your ability to use high level questions as part of the school's performance management procedures?*

  ☐ *out of 10*

- What evidence are you drawing upon in support of the grade that you have given yourself?

- What are the implications for your own development in this area?

Listening for meaning

- *How confident are you in your ability to listen for meaning as part of the school's performance management procedures?*

  ☐ *out of 10*

- What evidence are you drawing upon in support of the grade that you have given yourself?

- What are the implications for your own development in this area?

Being comfortable with a wide range of emotions

- *How confident are you in your ability to be comfortable with a wide range of emotions as part of the school's performance management procedures?*

  ☐ *out of 10*

- What evidence are you drawing upon in support of the grade that you have given yourself?

- What are the implications for your own development in this area?

_____

_____

Enabling staff to take ownership of objectives

- *How confident are you in your ability to enable staff to take ownership of goals set as part of the school's performance management procedures?*

  [ ] *out of 10*

- What evidence are you drawing upon in support of the grade that you have given yourself?

_____

_____

- What are the implications for your own development in this area?

_____

_____

Challenging staff to move out of their comfort zones

- *How confident are you in your ability to enable staff to move out of their comfort zones as part of the school's performance management procedures?*

  [ ] *out of 10*

- What evidence are you drawing upon in support of the grade that you have given yourself?

_____

_____

- What are the implications for your own development in this area?

_____

_____

Managing your own emotions

- *How confident are you in your ability to manage your own emotions as part of the school's performance management procedures?*

  ☐ out of 10

- What evidence are you drawing upon in support of the grade that you have given yourself?

_____

_____

- What are the implications for your own development in this area?

_____

_____

Building others' confidence and self-esteem

- *How confident are you in your ability to build others' confidence and self-esteem as part of the school's performance management procedures?*

  ☐ out of 10

- What evidence are you drawing upon in support of the grade that you have given yourself?

_____

_____

- What are the implications for your own development in this area?

_____

_____

Identifying others' limiting beliefs

- *How confident are you in your ability to enable others to overcome their self-limiting beliefs as part of the school's performance management procedures?*

  [ ] *out of 10*

- What evidence are you drawing upon in support of the grade that you have given yourself?

_____

_____

- What are the implications for your own development in this area?

_____

_____

CHAPTER 8:
Keeping Hope Alive

*Learn from yesterday,
live for today,
hope for tomorrow.*

**Albert Einstein
(Theoretical physicist and philosopher
of science)**

Keeping Hope Alive

In this chapter you will discover:
- Why hope and optimism are essential ingredients for the life of a school leader.
- How to keep hope at the centre of your leadership journey.
- The gaps in your own leadership survival kit and how to fill them.

Hope ... that stubborn thing inside of us that insists, despite all evidence to the contrary, that something better awaits us, so long as we have the courage to keep reaching, to keep working, to keep fighting.
Barack Obama

Hope

You would not have reached where you are now if you didn't know how to harness the power of hope. Hope not only in yourself, but also hope in the sincerity of your vision and the future that you are seeking to create for the children in your school. All school leaders need hope. Not just a spoonful of it – bags of it! This book has already shed light on why it is so tough to be a school leader today. This final chapter is dedicated to helping you discover how to keep refilling your bags of hope, so that you can both survive and thrive, and deliver the vision for all who seek to follow your lead.

The future we all seek – the future we want to create for our young people – can only be created if you know how to hold onto your hope, your vision, your values and the belief that you can – and you will – make things better for the young people in your school.

We all know hope can be incredibly elusive. When external demands and pressures mount and crisis follows crisis, the light at the end of the tunnel can appear to be a very faint and distant glimmer. In such times, hope is just as essential for our own well-being as rain is for flowers in the desert. From the ever-expanding self-help shelves in bookshops to the growing body of research from the field of social science, it is clear that hope is a human survival mechanism.

Hope, modern researchers are finding, does more than offer a bit of solace amidst affliction. It plays a surprisingly potent role in life, offering an advantage in realms as diverse as school achievement and bearing up in onerous jobs.
Goleman (1996)

As you seek to move forward and continue in your endeavour to create new and emboldened futures for our young people, I want to share with you seven lessons that I have discovered as a coach, which are essential for helping school leaders keep their hope alive.

Lesson 1—Learn to keep one eye backward and another eye forward

Here is a quote I came across a while ago, from Soren Kierkegaard:

Life can only be understood backwards, but it must be lived forwards.
Kierkegaard (Danish philosopher)

In essence, this is what reflection is about. In order to live more fully and to make progress with our lives, we need to have a process in place that enables us to develop a greater understanding of the journey, so that we can continue that journey with far deeper levels of insight and wisdom.

Throughout your life as a school leader, there will be moments when you can choose to start again. In the natural pauses of school life, there will be times when you can take learning from the past to create new, more aligned realities for yourself. They are, and should be, your personal times of both reflection and renewal.

We all learn to be ourselves though the process of living. It is paradoxical that we learn to be ourselves incidentally! The wider our experience of life and the more we learn to reflect on it and not take it for granted, the more we learn and the more we become whole people.
Jarvis (2005)

As you read the following case study, I'd like to invite you to think about two key questions:

1. What role does reflection play in your own life as a school leader?
2. How much of your leadership life to date has been influenced by your ability to look backwards?

CASE STUDY—Learning to look backwards: How coaching enabled an inner-city Headteacher to keep hope alive

The context
My coaching relationship with Grace, who had been a Headteacher for thirteen years, started nearly two years ago. She had spent eight years as the Headteacher of a two-form entry primary school.

Her school was situated in south London, with about 420 children and 60 staff. The children were from both very low and high income families, with a wide cultural and socioeconomic mix. The Free School Meal Entitlement was 53% – well above the national and local average. The percentage of pupils whose first language was not believed to be English was very high, at 31%. Approximately 20 languages were spoken in the school.

Grace's reasons for seeking coaching
'I decided to seek coaching after I received some training on how to be a coach. It was at that point that I realised how important it was for

me to have time to reflect within the working week, rather
than constantly giving such opportunities to other people. As an
experienced Headteacher I have been given many professional
development targets and opportunities, but felt that professional
reflection and dialogue with a coach would give me affirmation in
terms of my strengths as a leader, and would indicate those areas that
I would need to focus on in the future.'

A catalyst
'I have found the coaching relationship to be a catalyst for deep
personal and professional insight. The balance between challenge,
through searching questions and support through warmth, kindness
and humour has been crucial to the success of the relationship.'

The importance of systematic reflection
'Coaching has reminded me of the importance of systematic reflection.
This point alone has supported me as a Headteacher as I work through
the challenges of school leadership. It is changing the way myself and
my leadership team tackle challenges and celebrate our successes.
It has injected positivity into our dealings with children, staff and
parents, and has given me profound insights into staff struggling
with the roles that they find themselves in, and possible ways to
help them.'

Unpicking contradictions
'Coaching has enabled me to unpick the contradictions that I have
as a leader. I realised that I needed to give myself time to reflect
systematically, but needed to explore feelings of guilt about taking
that time. It has helped me unpick the accountability that I have as
a Headteacher, and has encouraged me to delegate responsibilities
away from myself.'

Maintaining personal well-being
'Above all, coaching has affirmed for me that, without personal
well-being, the role of leadership becomes even more difficult, and
therefore time taken to look after myself has had a major positive
impact on the quality of leadership that I am able to display and
sustain at school.

'Insights gained through coaching have enabled me to take some time away from school to both reflect and refresh myself educationally. I have also taken time away from school to deal with personal issues that in the past I would have compressed into my normal working life. My professional reading has increased which in turn has re-inspired and reinvigorated me as a leader.'

Optimism
'Whilst leading others, I am more conscious of being optimistic and positive in approach. I try to be affirmative and encouraging towards people who I would like to develop in a certain way. With people that are proving a challenge to lead/manage, I now think about the elements of well-being that may be having an impact on their performance/behaviour (career, health, relationships, finance, and place in the community). This has given me many insights into what their barriers may be, where they originate, and how best to support them. Management strategies that I am now consciously using include reflecting the issue back to the person and giving them the opportunity and permission to solve their own problems – before rushing to their aid!'

Through Grace's account we see that when we give time to ourselves and build in the practice of systematic reflection, we develop new habits and ways of being that are as of much benefit to ourselves as they are to those we lead and manage.

Lesson 2—Be connected

Leadership does not happen in a vacuum. Leaders need people, not only to follow them, but also to help them on their journey. The connections that you make as you move forward will have a great impact on the degree to which you are able to deal successfully with the challenges of school leadership. In school, and because of the nature of your role, relationships can often be one-dimensional, meaning that your total needs for human connection and relationship, as discussed in Chapter 1, can never be fully met while you wear the school leader 'hat'.

It might take a stretch of the imagination for you to believe this, but you do have a life outside your school! So it is important to invest in those other relationships that are beyond your life as a school leader. Actively search for relationships both within and outside your professional context that will:

- Affirm your self-worth.
- Give you constructive challenges.
- Open new learning opportunities.
- Allow you to be yourself.
- Create a space for you to be listened to.
- Enable you to be in a role where you are not expected to have all the answers!
- Provide a space for you to be taken care of and have your needs met.

Remember, you are a living, breathing, human being, not just your role!

Lesson 3—Learn the art of selfless leadership

We become our best selves through unselfish interaction with others.
Stengel (2010)

Growing up in the 1980s, I was very much involved in the anti-apartheid movement. When Mandela passed away in 2013, I felt as if I had lost a dearly loved family member. In an attempt to make sense of my feelings and what Mandela's life had meant to me, I returned to a book that I had read only a few years ago, *Mandela's Way: Lessons on Life* by Richard Stengel. Reflecting on Mandela's leadership, Stengel writes that:

The African model of leadership is better expressed as Ubuntu, the idea that people are empowered by other people, that we become our best selves through unselfish interaction with others.
Stengel (2010)

I'd like to think this is what coaching does. By putting aside one's ego and the perceived need to have all the answers, one can create a space in which a person is empowered through the simple acts of listening and the total giving of one's time and attention to the person they are with.

Ubuntu in action

My company trains school leaders so that they are able to gain a coaching qualification that will enable them to better support those that they lead and manage. As part of their training they have to complete a coaching diary, which is a record of their coaching sessions with their coachees.

CASE STUDY—How a deputy Headteacher put into practice the art of selfless leadership

Esther was a senior school leader on one of our training programmes, a deputy in a pupil referral unit. One of her coachees was Derek. Esther described him as: '... *a highly motivated and experienced teaching assistant (TA) who is currently asked to do over and above that of an ordinary TA. He is secure in his role and knowledge of the young people and the area we work in. However, Derek came to the profession from local supermarket retail about two years ago. While he has excelled and now realises that this is his area for a significant career, he has no formal qualifications to move on from the role of TA.'*

At the start of the coaching relationship Derek revealed to Esther that he had a very personal dream, which was to rise above the status of TA. Derek's opening line was: '*I want to teach my own lesson.'* *From that statement, he began to doubt himself, as he was almost embarrassed by saying out loud that he could even think of being a teacher.* As Esther reported: '*We held onto that and kept revisiting it.*

I questioned why he had never voiced this before. Derek spoke about his role as a rock. His family and friends always came to him with their issues and problems. Therefore Derek always pushed his own needs aside.'

In her role as coach, Esther was able to guide Derek through his self-doubt, so that by the time they reached their final session he was fully ready to seize his dream, as Esther says: *'It was clear from what Derek was saying that his mind was made up. Nothing would allow him to retreat from his goal. Pursuing his degree and going to college would make him and his family so proud and give him an intellectual/educational direction and challenge to his life.'*

Through coaching and selfless giving, Esther poignantly illustrates how the spirit of *Ubuntu* supports the development of others, restores hope, and empowers all who are a part of the process.

Esther's final reflections were: *'I was so much an advice-giver, wanting to help and solve problems. If I had been in that role, I would have totally limited this person. The goal came from him, so it was based on what he wanted – not my advice, which would have squashed his thoughts, expectations and dreams. This journey for Derek would never have happened if I had just carried on giving advice and not learnt how to coach.'*

When we embody the spirit of *Ubuntu*, we allow a person to connect with a higher vision of themselves. This is what Esther did with Derek. When people are supported to discover the gold inside of them, they discover for themselves the true meaning of hope and take positive steps to achieve their goal. They are happier and more motivated, and there is often a greater level of alignment between both their personal and professional aspirations.

Lesson 4—Bend, do not break

To cease to know what we feel is to cease to experience what things mean to us.
Branden (1994)

You may be familiar with the phrase 'bend, do not break', which some say has its origins either in one of Aesop's fables, The Olive Tree and the Reed, or an old Chinese proverb that relates to the capacity of the bamboo to bend (and not break) even in the severest of storms.

I would be lying (and indeed if you have been a school leader for long enough, you know that I would be lying) if I said you will never face any storms. The storms will come. Sometimes they will be a force nine gale, leaving a trail of human and emotional destruction in their wake; other times they will pass as quickly as they arrive, leaving only a few ruffled feathers. To survive them, you not only need to be anchored to your values, but you also need to know what resilience looks like for you.

For too many school leaders resilience has meant putting on a brave face while becoming detached from all feeling and emotion; they have become 'brittle' so that, when the storms come, they have forgotten what it means to 'bend'. They have no way of knowing how to respond to or listen to what their inner self, or indeed what other people, might be saying to help them survive the storm. They stand tall and rigid, only to be uprooted or snapped. And why does this happen?

When feelings and emotions are blocked and repressed, the process of implementation is physical; breathing is restricted and muscles contracted. When this happens repeatedly, the blocks become part of the body structure or 'the body armour'. Breathing may become so habitually shallow and the muscles so little contracted that the flow of feeling is obstructed and consciousness is diminished accordingly.
Branden (1994)

If you want to be able to withstand the storms of school leadership, you have to be able to bend. You have to be able to allow yourself to feel and, in so feeling, to be receptive to what your mind and your body are telling you – and take action that shows you have understood the message!

Lesson 5—Know that you have a choice

During everything that the life of a school leader throws at you, it is important to remember that you have a choice as to how you respond. When we understand this, we put our conscious selves back into the driving seat of our lives. We are in control of ourselves, as opposed to life's events and our emotions being in control of us.

In Nick Owen's book, *The Magic of Metaphor*, he shares an adaptation of an extract from *The Wind in the Willows* which illustrates the difference that awareness of and choice about our responses can make to our lives.

Mole was driving along a motorway with his friend, Badger. Mole was enjoying the drive and feeling good about the world until another car, driven by Rat, cut aggressively and dangerously in front of him. Mole was furious. He put his foot on the accelerator and chased after Rat, flashing, hooting and gesticulating. Mole was shouting and cursing, and purple with rage. Rat simply laughed to himself, made a rude gesture with his fingers, and accelerated away.

Mole was quite upset for the next hour. His day was spoilt. He felt frustrated and inadequate, as if his whole sense of masculinity had been called into question. He had been challenged and come off second-best. Badger had noticed his friend's behaviour but had chosen to say nothing for the time being. He waited until the time was right.

Finally Mole turned and said to him, 'That sort of driver makes me so angry.'

Badger replied, 'Forgive me, but I am really curious. How exactly do you allow yourself to get angry because of what another driver does?'

Mole was speechless. He had expected support. 'What do you mean?'

Badger said, 'What that other person did was simply information about him. How you responded is information about you. How exactly did you make yourself angry as a response to the other driver's behaviour?'

And so it was that Mole began to realise that he could choose his response to different situations. He could get angry if he wished, or stay calm and dismiss someone else's behaviour as information about them. It didn't have to affect him.

After that, Mole began to enjoy driving a lot more. Badger felt a lot safer in Mole's car, and Mole's wife noticed her husband was much less stressed and aggressive.

It's not always easy. It takes discipline and conscious effort to choose how we respond to life's calamities. However, when we master the art and become better at taking control of our lives, we experience the peace that comes in no longer letting others unduly influence our experience of living. We also restore hope in ourselves and promote it in those who are close to us.

Lesson 6—Laugh

Laugh – and laugh often! I know of no other place that provides such rich opportunities for laughter than a school. It's true, children say the funniest things. If you can't find humour in the things the children say, then look for it in the idiosyncrasies of your role. Goodness knows there are enough of them! If you are going to survive and thrive in this role, laughter has to be a part of your leadership survival kit. I don't believe you can do the job without it.

You need a healthy antidote to the pressures of school life and laughter is one of the best medicines around, with side effects that cause you no harm, but do an awful lot of good! Laughter reduces the flow of stress hormones such as cortisol and adrenaline and triggers the release of feel-good hormones and endorphins that help to promote an overall sense of health and well-being.

Laughter helps us keep an optimistic outlook through difficult situations, disappointment and loss. It helps us create a positive psychological distance from the cause of stress, thereby enabling us to see things from a new perspective. It gets us out of the present and restores overall balance, emotionally, mentally, spiritually and – if it's a good belly laugh – physically as well.

So when you find yourself weighed down by the pressures of school life:

- Find that one person in your school who you know will make you laugh.
- Reflect on moments in your career that have made you really smile or brought tears of laughter to your eyes.
- Recall things children have either said or done that have brightened your day.
- Do something that you enjoy outside of school that will cause you to put to one side the pressures of your role.

The impact will be far greater on your overall levels of hope and optimism than yet another read through of the new OFSTED Inspection framework!

Lesson 7—Capture the golden moments

They are there and they are precious. They are the parts of your life as a school leader that re-affirm why you do what you do in the school that you are in and for the community you serve. They are the parts of your school life that cause you to say at the end of each day *'That's the reason why I am here in this school, serving this community.'*

One of my key golden moments was listening to our school gospel choir sing on a Tuesday after school. At 4 o'clock I would walk into the school hall and there I would see Daniel, our charismatic choir master, bring his own unique blend of energy, laughter and musical wizardry into our school.

Amongst the many voices that sang out across the hall would be those of some of our most 'challenging' Year 6 boys, singing as though their lives depended on it. I would see the children proudly wearing gowns made from material that had been bought from the local market and made up by one of the parents. Support staff would step up as leaders and lead the children in song with Daniel. I would see Maggie, a stalwart of a parent from the local estate; she had very little money, but every Monday morning could be depended on to arrive at the staffroom door with her trolley of biscuits for all the staff. She would stand with her mum, whom I affectionately called Nan, and sing along with the children in the choir.

In those moments, even when I had had the toughest of days, I would immediately be connected back to my passion and purpose. The weight of the day would lift and, even if at times it was just a temporary lift, it was enough to help me to continue to strive forward with my vision for the school and the community we served.

Your golden moments will be unique for you and your school. Whatever you do, don't forget to collect them. As far as possible build them into either your daily, weekly or termly routine. They are the moments that will help to keep your flame of hope alive.

Over to you...

Undefended leaders are those who have learnt what it takes to face their own fears, doubts and uncertainties. They are people who have learnt the truth:

Courage is not the absence of fear, but the triumph over it.
Nelson Mandela (President of South Africa and anti-apartheid campaigner)

And that triumph over fear requires support, personal validation and a common understanding of the human vulnerabilities that we all share. These are the school leaders our children need: people who can model to both themselves and others what it means to be both vulnerable and courageous.

Our schools and our children do not need any more 'super-heads'. What our education system needs is school leaders with super hearts; those who have learnt to embrace the struggle of school leadership alongside the pursuit of the humanitarian goals of the 'undefended leader'. This concept illustrated in Figure 8.1.

Figure 8.1: The undefended leader
(adapted from Simon P. Walker, 2007)

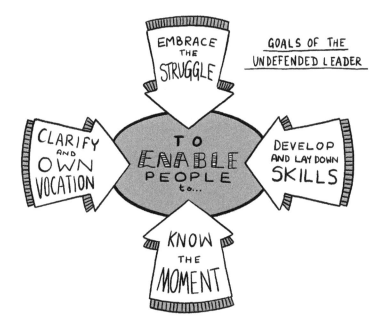

Time is a gift

Any worthwhile transformation does not happen overnight. A teacher does not become a successful, confident school leader overnight. It is a journey; it is a process – one that is very often uncomfortable and sometimes downright ugly on the inside.

Scientists tell us that if we were to open a chrysalis during a critical stage of the caterpillar's transformation, we would be shocked by what we would see. We would not see an embryonic butterfly or something that resembled some kind of insect life form; what we would find would be a liquidised, mixed up, vulnerable, unrecognisable mess. We would see caterpillar soup!

To the outside world, the cocoon gives the impression of wholeness, hiding the truth of what is actually occurring on the inside. And we have all done it! Kept up appearances, when on the inside everything was a complete and utter mixed-up mess!

Fortunately for us, nature does not look upon caterpillar soup as a culinary mistake and dismiss it as a recipe for failure. Nature knows that what the soup needs is patience and time. Without patience and time, neither we nor our children would ever know the beauty of butterflies.

If you are a school leader, the one thing you never seem to have enough of is time. Everything is urgent, and everything needs to have been 'done yesterday'. But if you are to both survive and thrive in your role, then time is a gift that you need to learn to be able to give to yourself. Just as nature affords time to the change process, school leaders need to have personal time invested in them as they learn to manage both the personal and external processes of school transformation.

That time will enable them to:

- Refill their emotional, mental and spiritual reservoirs.
- Embrace and develop new mechanisms for coping with the challenges of school leadership.
- Strengthen their inner foundations.
- Re-align themselves with all things, both personal and professional, that are of the greatest importance to them.

STOP, PAUSE AND REFLECT

I started this book with an exercise asking you to *begin with the end in mind*. I hope you are now a lot clearer about the 'end' that you wish for yourself, both personally and professionally. Now may be a good time for you to re-visit the two wheels at the beginning of the book and their accompanying questions. Then, in reflecting on the questions and what you have read in the pages of this book, ask yourself:

- Is there anything that I would change?
- Am I any clearer about how I will seek to achieve balance in my life as a school leader?
- Do I know the steps I will take to ensure that humanity and a commitment to high standards can walk as equal companions in my school?

The choice is yours. I hope you will chose wisely. Your future happiness and success, and our children's future happiness and success, will be shaped by the choices that you make.

REFERENCES

Arnold, K. Turner, N. and Barling, J. (2007) Transformational leadership and psychological well-being. *Journal of Occupational Health Psychology* 12(3), 193–203.

Boyatzis, R. and McKee, A. (2005) *Resonant Leadership*. USA: Harvard Business School Press.

Branden, N. (1994) *The Six Pillars of Self-Esteem*. USA: Bantam.

Brown, B. (2012) *Daring Greatly: How the Courage to be Vulnerable Transforms the Way we Live, Love, Parent and Lead*. London: Penguin.

Buck, A. (2009) *What Makes A Great School: A Practical Formula for Success*. London: National College for School Leadership.

Butler, G. and Hope, T. (2010) *Manage Your Mind: The Mental Fitness Guide*. London: Oxford University Press.

Cockman, P. Evans, B. and Reynolds, P. (2003) *Consulting for Real People*. London: McGraw-Hill.

Covey, S. (1989) *The Seven Habits of Highly Effective People*. UK: Simon and Schuster.

Dweck, C. (2012) *Mindset: How You Can Fulfil Your Potential*. London: Robinson.

Downey, M. (2003) *Effective Coaching*. USA: Thomson Texere.

Goleman, D. (1996) *Emotional Intelligence: Why It Can Matter More Than IQ*. London: Bloomsbury.

Goleman, D. (2003a) *Primal Leadership: The Hidden Driver of Great Performance*. USA: Harvard Business Press.

Goleman, D. (2003b) *The New Leaders*. USA: Sphere.

Harris, B. (2007) *Supporting the Emotional Work of School-Leaders*. London: Sage.

Harvard Business Review (2010) *On Managing Yourself*. USA: Harvard Business Review.

Hollis, J. (2006) *Finding Meaning in the Second Half of Life*. USA: Gotham Books.

Jarvis, P. (2005) *Towards a Comprehensive Theory of Human Learning*. London: Routledge.

Jay, J. (2009) *The Inner Edge: The 10 Practices of Personal Leadership*. USA: Praeger.

Lee, G. (2003) *Leadership Coaching*. London: Chartered Institute of Personal Development.

Lovewell, K. (2012) *Every Teacher Matters: Inspiring Well-Being Through Mindfulness*. UK: Ecademy Press.

Nichols, P. (2009) *The Lost Art of Listening: How Learning to Listen Can Improve Relationships*. USA: Guildford Press.

O'Conner, J. and Lages, A. (2007) *How Coaching Works*. London: A&C Black.

Owen, N. (2001) *The Magic of Metaphor: 77 Stories for Teachers, Trainers and Thinkers*. UK: Crown House.

Pask R. and Joy, B. (2007) *Mentoring–Coaching: A Guide for Education Professionals*. London: Open University Press.

Rogers, C.R. (1975) *Empathic: an unappreciated way of being*. The Counselling Psychologist, 5(2), 2–10.

Steele, C. (2001) *Whistling Vivaldi and Other Clues to How Stereotypes Affect Us*. USA: WW Norton.

Stengel, R. (2003) *Mandela's Way: Lessons on Life*. London: Virgin Books.

Walker, S.P. (2007) *Leading Out of Who You Are: Discovering the Secret of Undefended Leadership*. UK: Piquant Editions.

Lightning Source UK Ltd.
Milton Keynes UK
UKOW05f2331201016

285809UK00019B/873/P